JEREMIAH
BIBLE STUDY SERIES

1 & 2 THESSALONIANS

THE CALL TO A HOLY LIFE

DR. DAVID JEREMIAH

Prepared by Peachtree Publishing Services

THOMAS NELSON
Since 1798

1 & 2 THESSALONIANS
JEREMIAH BIBLE STUDY SERIES

© 2020 by Dr. David Jeremiah

Published in Nashville, Tennessee, by Thomas Nelson. Thomas Nelson is a registered trademark of HarperCollins Christian Publishing, Inc.

Produced with assistance of Peachtree Publishing Services (www.PeachtreePublishingServices.com). Project staff include Christopher D. Hudson and Randy Southern.

Thomas Nelson titles may be purchased in bulk for educational, business, fundraising, or sales promotional use. For information, please e-mail SpecialMarkets@ThomasNelson.com.

ISBN 978-0-310-09174-5 (softcover)
ISBN 978-0-310-09175-2 (ebook)

First Printing October 2020 / Printed in the United States of America

24 25 26 27 28 LBC 7 6 5 4 3

CONTENTS

INTRODUCTION TO
The Letters of 1 & 2 Thessalonians

"From you the word of the Lord has sounded forth, not only in Macedonia and Achaia, but also in every place. Your faith toward God has gone out, so that we do not need to say anything" (1 Thessalonians 1:8). One of the greatest joys the apostle Paul must have experienced was in witnessing those whom he discipled surpassing his expectations. Such was the case with the believers in Thessalonica. They were surviving—and thriving—under the worst conditions. In the midst of persecution and suffering, these believers were spreading the gospel so quickly and effectively that it was making Paul's ministry unnecessary in certain places. Paul's joy, excitement, and gratitude are evident throughout his letters to the Thessalonians. But his need to correct false teachings they had adopted—such as wrong beliefs about Jesus' return—is also evident in his words. Paul's letters thus serve as an encouragement for the believers in Thessalonica—and for us—to keep sharing the gospel . . . but to do so with sound doctrine.

1 THESSALONIANS

Author and Date

The author of this letter identifies himself as Paul (see 1:1), and his opening words indicate that he wrote it alongside two close associates: Timothy (his coworker) and Silvanus (also known as Silas). The epistle contains a number of details about Paul's life that fit with what we know of him based on his other letters and the book of Acts—particularly the events of Paul's experience in Thessalonica as recorded in Acts 17:1–9. The early Muratorian Canon (c. AD 180) listed the epistle as among Paul's works, and early church leaders such as Irenaeus (c. AD 185), Tertullian (c. AD 210), and Clement of Alexandria (c. AD 198) all acknowledged it was authored by the apostle. It is likely Paul wrote 1 Thessalonians during his stay in Corinth, c. AD 50.

Background and Setting

Paul arrived in Thessalonica during his second missionary journey, c. AD 49–50, and likely ministered in the city for several months. Luke records he was accompanied by Silas, and they began preaching the gospel in the Jewish synagogue, "explaining and demonstrating that the Christ had to suffer and rise again from the dead" (Acts 17:3). The message resonated with a few Jewish men, many devout Greeks (Gentiles), and some of the leading women in the city. Unfortunately, this triggered an angry reaction among the Thessalonian Jews, and ultimately they formed a mob and drove the men from the city. The two escaped to Berea, but were also forced to flee that city when the mob followed them. Paul eventually made his way to Corinth, where he sent his coworker Timothy to check on the believers in Thessalonica. The report Paul received back gladdened his heart, prompting him to write his first letter to express his joy and thankfulness that the community was thriving in spite of persecution. Paul also took the opportunity to defend himself against certain false accusations, explain why he had not yet returned to the city himself, and correct some doctrinal errors that had surfaced.

Key Themes

Several key themes are prominent in Paul's first letter to the Thessalonians. The first is that *believers in Christ must persevere in their faith*. The believers in Thessalonica were facing persecution for their decision to follow Christ as their Savior. Paul is concerned they might turn away from the message of the gospel in the midst of that pressure, so he expresses his thankfulness for them and encourages them to keep "setting the example" for others in their faith. Paul wants them to know he has not forgotten about them. In fact, he longs to be with them again so he can help them to mature spiritually (see 1 Thessalonians 1:1–10; 2:17–20).

A second theme is that *followers of Christ must remember their high calling.* Paul's opponents in Thessalonica were calling his conduct into question, and he was concerned these attacks might cause some to question the gospel he was proclaiming. So, Paul defends himself by explaining his true motives and the work God has for him to do (see 2:1–12). In the process, he reminds the believers of their high calling from God and urges them to pursue lives of holiness, extend brotherly love to one another, and continue making God-honoring choices in their lives (see 4:1–12).

A third theme is that *believers in Jesus can look forward to the return of Christ.* In Paul's absence, the believers in Thessalonica were raising questions about the return of Christ into this world. This appears to have been prompted by the fact that many in the congregation had died—and they were concerned that these believers would "miss out" and not participate in the resurrection. Paul encourages them by stating that these believers who have "fallen asleep" will actually rise first and be caught up with those who are still living. In this way, they can—and should—look forward with hope to this coming future event (see 4:13–5:11).

2 THESSALONIANS

Author and Date

The author of this letter also identifies himself as Paul (see 1:1), and his opening words again indicate he was collaborating in the writing of the letter with his associates Timothy and Silas. The epistle contains a number of clarifications from Paul on points raised in his first letter, indicating the apostle is responding to questions and concerns the believers in Thessalonica had raised after receiving it. Furthermore, early church leaders such as Irenaeus (c. AD 185), Tertullian (c. AD 210), and Clement of Alexandria (c. AD 198) acknowledged it was authored by Paul. It is likely Paul wrote 2 Thessalonians during his same stay in Corinth, c. AD 51–52.

Background and Setting

Paul's concern for the congregation in Thessalonica did not end after sending his first letter to them. Shortly after dispatching that epistle, the apostle evidently received word of troubling developments that had taken place in the community. The persecution of the church members had increased, and many now believed they were in the midst of the day of the Lord and experiencing the events of the Tribulation. Furthermore, some in the community had given up work and other responsibilities so they could sit idly by and "wait" for the Lord's return. Paul needed to correct these misunderstandings and compel the believers to not give up on their calling, their work, or their duties to one another in the faith.

Key Themes

Several key themes are prominent in Paul's second letter to the Thessalonians. The first is that *believers in Christ will endure suffering at times for God's kingdom*. Paul acknowledges in his opening words that the believers in Thessalonica are suffering persecutions for "the kingdom of God" (2 Thessalonians 1:5). He prays that God will "repay with tribulation" those who are persecuting them and that He will give them rest (verse 7). He reminds the church that trials in this world are momentary, but the blessings they will receive if they endure in the faith will be eternal. Their response must be to continue in faithfulness, patience, and endurance as they look forward to the return of Jesus (see verses 9–10).

A second theme is that *believers must be wary of the enemy's deceptions*. As previously noted, a false report had surfaced among the church members that the suffering they were enduring was a sign the great Tribulation had begun. Paul is compelled to correct this deception of the enemy by reminding the believers of the sound doctrine he taught when he was with them. Notably, he reminds them the "man of sin" must first be revealed—and this cannot occur until "He who now restrains" allows him to do so (see 2:1–12). For this reason, the believers are to "stand fast and hold the traditions" that they were taught (verse 15).

A third theme is that *believers need to remain busy doing God's work*. Paul ends his letter with a rebuke to those in the church who had decided to stop working so they could sit idly by and wait for Jesus to return. Paul reminds the believers of how he and his colleagues conducted themselves when they were in their midst—not by taking handouts, as was their right, but by working diligently. In the same manner, the believers were to "get busy" doing the work that God had called them to do and never become weary in doing good (see 3:6–15).

KEY APPLICATIONS

The life of a Christian more closely resembles that of a *marathon* than a *sprint*. In this world, we will experience setbacks, challenges, and trials that will tempt us to go off course and slow our pace. During such times, the apostle Paul encourages us to cling to the promises found in God's Word. We must remember that while trials in this life are temporary, the reward for our perseverance is eternal life with our heavenly Father. For this reason, we must cling to the truths we have been taught and not be deceived by lies from the enemy. We must keep our eyes fixed on God's Word, knowing what it says and doesn't say so no one can lead us astray.

A DYNAMIC CHURCH

1 Thessalonians 1:1–10

GETTING STARTED

Who has served as an example of what it means to follow Jesus? What did that person do that compelled you to want to follow his or her example?

_____

_____

_____

_____

_____

_____

_____

_____

_____

_____

_____

_____

SETTING THE STAGE

In the book of Acts, Luke writes that Paul, Silas, and Timothy traveled to Philippi when Paul received a vision of a man of Macedonia pleading with him for help (see Acts 16:6–12). After encouraging the believers in Philippi for a few days, Paul and his ministry team headed for Thessalonica, one of the few cities of the Bible that can be visited today. In the apostle's day, there were 200,000 people living in the city. Most of the inhabitants were Greeks, but there was also a large Roman contingent and a strong Jewish community in the city.

When Paul arrived, he first preached the message of the gospel in the local Jewish synagogue. As a result of his efforts, some of the Jews, a "multitude" of the Greeks, and many prominent women received the message of hope proclaimed to them. For them, Paul's message did not represent another philosophical discussion or debate—as was so prevalent among the many scholars in the city. Rather, it was a strong, penetrating, life-altering presentation of the gospel of Jesus Christ that came in the power of the Holy Spirit (see Acts 17:1–4).

It is unclear how long Paul remained in Thessalonica. However, it was long enough for him to receive two offerings from the Philippians (see Philippians 4:16), engage in gainful employment (see 1 Thessalonians 2:9), and leave behind a thriving community when he was finally forced to leave at the hands of an angry Jewish mob (see Acts 17:5–9). During that time—however long it might have been—it is evident that Paul was preaching the Word of God, answering the people's questions about Christ, and building the nucleus of this church.

EXPLORING THE TEXT

Paul's Greeting (1 Thessalonians 1:1–5)

¹ Paul, Silvanus, and Timothy,

To the church of the Thessalonians in God the Father and the Lord Jesus Christ:

Grace to you and peace from God our Father and the Lord Jesus Christ.

² We give thanks to God always for you all, making mention of you in our prayers, ³ remembering without ceasing your work of

faith, labor of love, and patience of hope in our Lord Jesus Christ in the sight of our God and Father, [4] knowing, beloved brethren, your election by God. [5] For our gospel did not come to you in word only, but also in power, and in the Holy Spirit and in much assurance, as you know what kind of men we were among you for your sake.

---

1. Paul mentions in his opening that he is writing this letter with his coworkers Silas (Silvanus) and Timothy—an important distinction given that he will soon ask the Thessalonians to remember the work that he *and* his team did in their midst. Why does Paul then say he is thankful for the Thessalonian believers (see verses 2–3)?

_____

_____

_____

_____

_____

2. Paul describes the believers as "beloved" and mentions their "election by God" (see verse 4). His words reflect what Moses told the people of Israel: "The LORD did not set His love on you nor choose you because you were more in number than any other people . . . but because the LORD loves you" (Deuteronomy 7:7–8). How does Paul assure the believers of their status as God's elect—as God's chosen people (see verses 4–5)?

_____

_____

_____

_____

The Thessalonian Believers' Good Example
(1 Thessalonians 1:6–10)

⁶ And you became followers of us and of the Lord, having received the word in much affliction, with joy of the Holy Spirit, ⁷ so that you became examples to all in Macedonia and Achaia who believe. ⁸ For from you the word of the Lord has sounded forth, not only in Macedonia and Achaia, but also in every place. Your faith toward God has gone out, so that we do not need to say anything. ⁹ For they themselves declare concerning us what manner of entry we had to you, and how you turned to God from idols to serve the living and true God, ¹⁰ and to wait for His Son from heaven, whom He raised from the dead, even Jesus who delivers us from the wrath to come.

3. When the Thessalonian believers received the gospel, they suffered "much affliction" in their relationships (verse 6). Their decision to follow Christ would have caused them to be ostracized from friends and family members and excluded from certain social events. But rather than continue in their former habits and activities, they began to imitate Paul and those who traveled with him. How did the Thessalonian believers become examples to other believers throughout the whole Mediterranean region (verses 6–8)?

4. Paul describes the Thessalonian believers as turning from "idols," which reveals that most of the congregation had come from a Gentile background. (At this time, the Jews would not have practiced overt forms of idolatry.) What were they now doing instead (see verses 9–10)?

_____

_____

_____

_____

_____

_____

_____

GOING DEEPER

In the book of Acts, we read that Paul and Silas came to Thessalonica after being beaten in Philippi and basically run out of the city (see 16:16–40). It must have been a long and painful journey for the two men, but their efforts were quickly rewarded when Paul began preaching the gospel in the local Jewish synagogue. Luke relates how the church was founded—and the uproar that followed when the Jewish contingent in the city stirred up trouble against them.

Preaching Christ at Thessalonica (Acts 17:1–9)

¹ Now when they had passed through Amphipolis and Apollonia, they came to Thessalonica, where there was a synagogue of the Jews. ² Then Paul, as his custom was, went in to them, and for three Sabbaths reasoned with them from the Scriptures, ³ explaining and demonstrating that the Christ had to suffer and rise again from the dead, and saying, "This Jesus whom I preach to you is the Christ." ⁴ And some of them were persuaded; and a great multitude of the devout Greeks, and not a few of the leading women, joined Paul and Silas.

⁵ But the Jews who were not persuaded, becoming envious, took some of the evil men from the marketplace, and gathering a mob, set all the city in an uproar and attacked the house of Jason, and sought to bring them out to the people. ⁶ But when they did not find them, they dragged Jason and some brethren to the rulers of the city, crying out, "These who have turned the world upside down have come here too. ⁷ Jason has harbored them, and these are all acting contrary to the decrees of Caesar, saying there is another king—Jesus." ⁸ And they troubled the crowd and the rulers of the city when they heard these things. ⁹ So when they had taken security from Jason and the rest, they let them go.

5. What plan did the unbelieving Jews devise to capture Paul and Silas? What does Luke say motivated their behavior (see verses 1–5)?

_____

_____

_____

_____

_____

6. How did the Thessalonians who opposed Paul and Silas and their ministry describe Christians? What did they accuse the Christians of doing (see verses 6–7)?

_____

_____

_____

_____

_____

Jason and his family escaped execution at the hands of the authorities. Paul and Silas, not wanting to put them at further risk, decided to escape the city by night and head to nearby Berea. However, their opponents in Thessalonica soon followed to disrupt their ministry there.

Ministering at Berea (Acts 17:10–15)

[10] Then the brethren immediately sent Paul and Silas away by night to Berea. When they arrived, they went into the synagogue of the Jews. [11] These were more fair-minded than those in Thessalonica, in that they received the word with all readiness, and searched the Scriptures daily to find out whether these things were so. [12] Therefore many of them believed, and also not a few of the Greeks, prominent women as well as men. [13] But when the Jews from Thessalonica learned that the word of God was preached by Paul at Berea, they came there also and stirred up the crowds. [14] Then immediately the brethren sent Paul away, to go to the sea; but both Silas and Timothy remained there. [15] So those who conducted Paul brought him to Athens; and receiving a command for Silas and Timothy to come to him with all speed, they departed.

7. What kind of reception did Paul and Silas receive in Berea (see verses 10–12)?

8. How did the believers in Berea react when the troublemakers from Thessalonica showed up (see verses 13–15)?

_____

_____

_____

_____

_____

_____

REVIEWING THE STORY

Paul begins his letter by expressing his prayers for the believers in Thessalonica. He gives thanks for their extraordinary witness and their ability to maintain a spirit of faith, love, and hope in the midst of troubling circumstances. He remarks how their first concern has never been for themselves or their own welfare but for God's will to be accomplished and His kingdom to be furthered. He notes how the dramatic change in the lives of the believers has served as an inspiration to believers and unbelievers throughout the region. The church in Thessalonica has thrived because it focused not on its present circumstances but on the coming of Christ.

9. What was Paul's attitude toward the church in Thessalonica (see 1 Thessalonians 1:2)?

_____

_____

_____

_____

_____

_____

10. How were the Thessalonian believers able to maintain hope in the midst of troubling times (see 1 Thessalonians 1:4)?

_____

_____

_____

_____

_____

_____

11. How had the gospel of Christ come to the Thessalonians (see 1 Thessalonians 1:5)?

_____

_____

_____

_____

_____

_____

12. What impact did the outreach and evangelism of the Thessalonian believers have on the territory around them (see 1 Thessalonians 1:8)?

_____

_____

_____

_____

_____

APPLYING THE MESSAGE

13. How do you respond to the idea that God has chosen you to fulfill a specific purpose?

_____

_____

_____

_____

_____

_____

_____

_____

14. In what areas do you need greater endurance to fulfill that purpose from God?

_____

_____

_____

_____

_____

_____

_____

_____

REFLECTING ON THE MEANING

The apostle Paul opens his first letter to the believers in Thessalonica with the statement, "We give thanks to God always for you all, making mention of you in our prayers, remembering without ceasing your work of faith, labor of love, and patience of hope in our Lord Jesus Christ in the sight of our God and Father" (1 Thessalonians 1:2–3). Paul's words reveal three important traits these believers possessed that we also need to have in our lives.

First, they had a faith that was alive. Paul remembers their "work of faith" (verse 3). It is an interesting phase, for typically we view the terms *work* and *faith* as being opposites of one another. We don't perceive the two as belonging to the same category. But they do! A *work of faith* had led them to accept the message of the gospel in the first place. Now, it was providing the motivation for them to continue in the faith and serve the Lord. It was the *work of faith* within them that caused all of these things to happen. Their faith was alive.

Second, they had a love that was active. Paul says that he remembers their "labor of love" (verse 3). If we truly love others, we are willing to engage in labor on behalf of that person. We are willing to minister to them and express our love to them. The Thessalonian believers had an active love. Paul goes on to explain this had led them to stand with him: "You became followers of us and of the Lord, having received the word in much affliction, with joy of the Holy Spirit" (verse 6). The active love they possessed led them to follow Paul's example, dedicate themselves to the Lord, and delight in God's Word.

Third, they had a hope that was abundant. Paul recalls not only their "work of faith" and their "labor of love," but also their "patience of hope in our Lord Jesus Christ in the sight of our God and Father" (verse 3). The believers had a *sustaining* hope (for it was patient), a *sure* hope (for it was grounded in the Lord Jesus), and a *sincere* hope (because it was in the sight of God). As we continue to explore Paul's words in these epistles, we will discover that he frequently writes to the Thessalonians about hope—hope in Jesus' return, hope in the resurrection, and hope for those still living who were facing persecution for their faith. It was a message that the Thessalonians needed to hear . . . and one that we need to hear as well.

JOURNALING YOUR RESPONSE

How are you preparing for the opposition you will face as you work to expand the borders of God's kingdom?

HALLMARKS OF AUTHENTIC MINISTRY

1 Thessalonians 2:1–12

GETTING STARTED

What is the danger in seeking approval from others when it comes to your ministry for Christ?

_____

_____

_____

_____

_____

_____

_____

_____

_____

_____

SETTING THE STAGE

Paul engaged in a wide range of Christian service during his ministry. In this next section, he reveals some of the work that he did among the believers in Thessalonica—and, by extension, the kind of work that *we* should be doing as we serve God. What is striking is the way Paul sets up this discussion of his ministry by first describing it using negative terms. In the first six verses of 1 Thessalonians 2, he mentions nine ways *not* to do ministry.

Sometimes, it is important to first tell people what were are *not* going to do and *not* going to say before we get to what we *are* actually going to do and say. Paul recognized that his opponents were undermining his efforts in the congregation and questioning his motives. So, he needed to state that his ministry was not *vain*, nor based in *error*, in *uncleanness*, or in *deceit*. His ministry was not meant to *please people*. He did not employ *flattering words*, used as a *cloak of covetousness*, to seek *glory from them* or *glory from others*. Paul's words offer an important grid through which we can examine our own service for Christ. If we serve the Lord with any of those attitudes, we are not doing the work of ministry as we should.

Paul then makes five positive statements about how we *should* do ministry in the next six verses. Our ministry should exhibit *gentleness*. If we are called on to serve, we are to have the same spirit that a mother has for her children. Our ministry should also *impart the gospel* to others—through not only our words but also our example. We should be willing to *share our lives* with those whom we serve. We are to conduct ourselves *justly and blamelessly*. Finally, we are to *exhort, comfort, and charge* others to follow after Christ. We need not only the tenderness of a nursing mother but the strength of a concerned father (see verses 7–12).

As we serve others in ministry, we must do so for the same reason as Paul served—so that others will "walk worthy of God," who calls them into His kingdom (verse 12).

EXPLORING THE TEXT

Paul's Conduct in Thessalonica (1 Thessalonians 2:1–6)

---

¹ For you yourselves know, brethren, that our coming to you was not in vain. ² But even after we had suffered before and were spitefully treated at Philippi, as you know, we were bold in our God to speak

to you the gospel of God in much conflict. ³ For our exhortation did not come from error or uncleanness, nor was it in deceit.

⁴ But as we have been approved by God to be entrusted with the gospel, even so we speak, not as pleasing men, but God who tests our hearts. ⁵ For neither at any time did we use flattering words, as you know, nor a cloak for covetousness—God is witness. ⁶ Nor did we seek glory from men, either from you or from others, when we might have made demands as apostles of Christ.

---

1. Luke writes that Paul and Silas were accused by the Jews in Thessalonica of "acting contrary to the decrees of Caesar, saying there is another king—Jesus" (Acts 17:7). However, this accusation did not stop Paul and Silas from boldly proclaiming the gospel in that city. According to Paul, what gave him and his companions the courage to continue proclaiming the gospel even when facing accusations and maltreatment (see 1 Thessalonians 2:2–4)?

_____

_____

_____

_____

_____

2. Paul's opponents often liked to challenge his motives and imply that he did not have his congregations' best interests at heart. What evidence does Paul present to defend himself and his companions from any accusation that the message they proclaimed in Thessalonica was an attempt at deceiving people or attaining self-praise (see verses 5–6)?

_____

_____

_____

_____

_____

Paul's Defense of His Behavior (1 Thessalonians 2:7–12)

7 But we were gentle among you, just as a nursing mother cherishes her own children. 8 So, affectionately longing for you, we were well pleased to impart to you not only the gospel of God, but also our own lives, because you had become dear to us. 9 For you remember, brethren, our labor and toil; for laboring night and day, that we might not be a burden to any of you, we preached to you the gospel of God.

10 You are witnesses, and God also, how devoutly and justly and blamelessly we behaved ourselves among you who believe; 11 as you know how we exhorted, and comforted, and charged every one of you, as a father does his own children, 12 that you would walk worthy of God who calls you into His own kingdom and glory.

3. Paul and his companions had the right to demand things such as respect and payment from the Thessalonian believers (see 1 Corinthians 9:3–18). However, as Paul notes in this passage, they chose *not* to exert their authority or line their pockets. What approach did they take instead? Why did they take this approach (see 1 Thessalonians 2:7–9)?

_____

_____

_____

_____

_____

_____

_____

_____

_____

_____

4. Paul and his companions could say they acted "blamelessly" in the sight of God and in the presence of the believers (verse 10). What are some of the actions they exemplified? How did they expect the believers in Thessalonica to respond (see verses 11–12)?

_____

_____

_____

_____

_____

_____

GOING DEEPER

Paul opens this section of his letter by reminding the believers how he and Silas "had suffered before and were spitefully treated at Philippi" (1 Thessalonians 2:2). Luke provides greater detail and background information in the book of Acts as to the cause of this suffering. As he notes, it all began with the exorcism of a demon from a slave girl in that city.

Paul and Silas Imprisoned in Philippi (Acts 16:16–24)

16 Now it happened, as we went to prayer, that a certain slave girl possessed with a spirit of divination met us, who brought her masters much profit by fortune-telling. 17 This girl followed Paul and us, and cried out, saying, "These men are the servants of the Most High God, who proclaim to us the way of salvation." 18 And this she did for many days.

But Paul, greatly annoyed, turned and said to the spirit, "I command you in the name of Jesus Christ to come out of her." And he came out that very hour. 19 But when her masters saw that their hope of profit was gone, they seized Paul and Silas and dragged them into the marketplace to the authorities.

²⁰ And they brought them to the magistrates, and said, "These men, being Jews, exceedingly trouble our city; ²¹ and they teach customs which are not lawful for us, being Romans, to receive or observe." ²² Then the multitude rose up together against them; and the magistrates tore off their clothes and commanded them to be beaten with rods. ²³ And when they had laid many stripes on them, they threw them into prison, commanding the jailer to keep them securely. ²⁴ Having received such a charge, he put them into the inner prison and fastened their feet in the stocks.

---

5. What prompted Paul to command the demonic spirit to leave the girl? What was the real reason people were upset by his healing of the slave girl (see verses 16–19)?

_____

_____

_____

_____

_____

6. What did Paul and Silas receive as a result of their selfless efforts to heal the slave girl and proclaim the way of salvation in Philippi (see verses 22–24)?

_____

_____

_____

_____

_____

_____

Paul reveals in his letters that one way he kept his ministry above reproach was to work at his trade as a tentmaker to support himself financially. In this way, he was free to speak God's truth without worrying about offending any benefactors. In his first letter to the Corinthians, he explains why he never claimed the right to the financial support that was due him as an apostle.

A Pattern of Self-Denial (1 Corinthians 9:3–14)

[3] My defense to those who examine me is this: [4] Do we have no right to eat and drink? [5] Do we have no right to take along a believing wife, as do also the other apostles, the brothers of the Lord, and Cephas? [6] Or is it only Barnabas and I who have no right to refrain from working? [7] Who ever goes to war at his own expense? Who plants a vineyard and does not eat of its fruit? Or who tends a flock and does not drink of the milk of the flock?

[8] Do I say these things as a mere man? Or does not the law say the same also? [9] For it is written in the law of Moses, "You shall not muzzle an ox while it treads out the grain." Is it oxen God is concerned about? [10] Or does He say it altogether for our sakes? For our sakes, no doubt, this is written, that he who plows should plow in hope, and he who threshes in hope should be partaker of his hope. [11] If we have sown spiritual things for you, is it a great thing if we reap your material things? [12] If others are partakers of this right over you, are we not even more?

Nevertheless we have not used this right, but endure all things lest we hinder the gospel of Christ. [13] Do you not know that those who minister the holy things eat of the things of the temple, and those who serve at the altar partake of the offerings of the altar? [14] Even so the Lord has commanded that those who preach the gospel should live from the gospel.

7. Paul was defending himself in this passage against those who questioned the legitimacy of his apostolic authority because he refused to accept payment for his services. Some of the other apostles traveled with their wives and received food, drink, and financial support from the churches in which they ministered. What does Paul say about those who have "sown spiritual things" for others (see verses 11–12)?

_____

_____

_____

_____

8. Although Paul had the right to be given payment for his preaching and ministry among the Corinthian believers (see verses 3–12, 14), he chose not to make use of his right. Why does Paul say he refused to demand this right as an apostle (see verse 12)?

_____

_____

_____

_____

_____

REVIEWING THE STORY

Paul defends his conduct among the Thessalonian believers by reminding them of how he arrived to them after enduring persecution in Philippi. He notes that in spite of the trials he faced (which included beatings and imprisonment), he was bold in presenting the gospel to them. Paul states that his aim has always been to please God, not people, and that he has never resorted to flattery or false claims in making his case for the gospel. He reminds the believers that he and Silas conducted themselves blamelessly among them and urges them to follow their example and do the same when they seek to spread the gospel.

9. How did Paul and Silas demonstrate their boldness in Thessalonica (see 1 Thessalonians 2:2)?

_____

_____

_____

_____

_____

10. What did Paul and Silas refuse to do as they presented the gospel to the Thessalonians (see 1 Thessalonians 2:5–6)?

_____

_____

_____

_____

11. What did Paul want the Thessalonian believers to remember about his time with them (see 1 Thessalonians 2:9)?

_____

_____

_____

_____

12. What kind of behavior did Paul and Silas exhibit when they were with the Christians in Thessalonica (see 1 Thessalonians 2:10–12)?

_____

_____

_____

_____

_____

APPLYING THE MESSAGE

13. What unique experiences have you had in defending your words or actions as a follower of Christ?

_____

_____

_____

_____

_____

14. How can you incorporate Paul's example of evangelism into your own presentation of the gospel?

_____

_____

_____

_____

REFLECTING ON THE MEANING

In this section of Paul's letter, we get insights directly from the apostle on how he viewed his ministry and how he conducted himself in his work to spread the message of Christ. As we noted, he first lists all of the things that we _not_ do when we seek to serve. But then he moves on to all of the things that we _should_ be doing as we serve. From his words, we can identify six mindsets that we need to adopt if we want to be effective in our roles.

First, we must be _courageous_, like good soldiers. Paul wrote, "Even after we had suffered . . . we were bold in our God to speak to you the gospel of God in much conflict" (1 Thessalonians 2:2). He was bold in his presentation of the gospel, even though he had just faced persecution in Philippi. He refused to be defeated or discouraged.

Second, we must be *conscientious*, like wise stewards. Paul said, "We have been approved by God to be entrusted with the gospel" (verse 4). He understood the Lord had given him the gospel to carefully steward and administer to others. This is an awesome trust—and one that we can never take lightly. As stewards, we must make sure that the gospel is presented courageously, clearly, and convincingly.

Third, we must be *cautious*, like gracious servants. Paul stated, "We speak, not as pleasing men, but God who tests our hearts" (verse 4). Paul did not seek human honor or acceptance. He put aside any worldly ambitions and refused to seek worldly glory. He followed the example of Christ, who told His disciples, "The Son of Man did not come to be served, but to serve, and to give His life a ransom for many" (Matthew 20:28).

Fourth, we must be *comforting*, like a godly mother. Paul wrote of his conduct toward the Thessalonians, "We were gentle among you, just as a nursing mother cherishes her own children" (1 Thessalonians 2:7). Once a child is born, a mother is on call twenty-four hours a day. She is often exhausted but does not allow that to derail her efforts to care for her child. This is how Paul states that we are to minister to one another in the family of God.

Fifth, we must be *careful*, so we might set a godly example. Paul called the believers in Thessalonica to "remember . . . how devoutly and justly and blamelessly we behaved ourselves among you who believe" (verses 9–10). Paul was referring here not just to the attitude he adopted but also the example he set. The standard is high for those who desire to serve.

Sixth, we must be *concerned*, like a caring father. Paul wrote, "We exhorted, and comforted, and charged every one of you, as a father does his own children" (verse 11). A father challenges his child when it is needed. He puts his arm around his child and says, "We can get through this. You're going to be okay." He gives instruction and direction. In the same way, we are to urge others forward when they need to pursue a course of action.

Paul's goal was to help others "walk worthy of God" (verse 12). This must be our aim in ministry as well—whether in teaching, leadership, or service. We never know whose eyes are watching us, whose ears are listening to us, and whose hearts are opening to the gospel.

Journaling Your Response

How are you setting an example for new believers in the way that you minister to others?

_____

_____

_____

_____

_____

_____

_____

_____

_____

_____

_____

_____

_____

_____

_____

_____

_____

_____

_____

_____

_____

_____

A SHARED EXPERIENCE OF SUFFERING

1 Thessalonians 2:13–20

GETTING STARTED

What good has come from an experience of suffering in your life?

_____

_____

_____

_____

_____

_____

_____

_____

_____

_____

_____

_____

_____

_____

_____

_____

_____

_____

_____

_____

_____

SETTING THE STAGE

History reveals that some of the greatest growth spurts in the church have occurred during the most challenging times. Faith often flourishes during moments of intense persecution. This was true as far back as the days of the early church, when a great persecution broke out against the church in Jerusalem (see Acts 8:1–8). The disciples continued to preach Christ as they fled, and as a result the gospel spread to places such as Samaria and beyond.

The apostle Paul was aware of the persecution the believers in Thessalonica were facing because of their faith in Christ. He understood the nature of their suffering—for he had also been persecuted in that city. He knew the hostility of those who were opposed to the spread of the gospel—a hostility that had once taken up residence in his own heart before his conversion (see Galatians 1:22–23). In fact, it was Paul (then known as Saul) who had led the charge against the early believers in Jerusalem.

In this section of Paul's letter, he commends the Thessalonian believers for their faith. They had withstood many tests and continued to sound the gospel. Remember, this was the church that had exceeded Paul's expectations in evangelism. But this outreach had come not in a climate of peace and tranquility but one of persecution and suffering. The believers—much like Paul himself—had allowed adversity to be a motivating factor in their lives. We must do the same.

EXPLORING THE TEXT

The Faith of the Thessalonians (1 Thessalonians 2:13–16)

¹³ For this reason we also thank God without ceasing, because when you received the word of God which you heard from us, you welcomed it not as the word of men, but as it is in truth, the word of God, which also effectively works in you who believe. ¹⁴ For you, brethren, became imitators of the churches of God which are in Judea in Christ Jesus. For you also suffered the same things from your own countrymen, just as

they did from the Judeans, [15] who killed both the Lord Jesus and their own prophets, and have persecuted us; and they do not please God and are contrary to all men, [16] forbidding us to speak to the Gentiles that they may be saved, so as always to fill up the measure of their sins; but wrath has come upon them to the uttermost.

1. In these verses, Paul expresses thanksgiving for the Thessalonian believers' acceptance of "the word of God" (verse 13). How does Paul say they had received this word?

_____

_____

_____

_____

_____

_____

2. In Paul's letters, we find that he generally stays positive when speaking of his fellow Jews, as he desires them to come to faith in Christ. In this passage, however, he directs harsh criticism at them and warns of God's inescapable wrath on those who reject Jesus and the gospel. What charges does Paul bring against those Jews in this passage (see verses 14–16)?

_____

_____

_____

_____

_____

_____

_____

Paul's Longing to Return (1 Thessalonians 2:17–20)

¹⁷ But we, brethren, having been taken away from you for a short time in presence, not in heart, endeavored more eagerly to see your face with great desire. ¹⁸ Therefore we wanted to come to you—even I, Paul, time and again—but Satan hindered us. ¹⁹ For what is our hope, or joy, or crown of rejoicing? Is it not even you in the presence of our Lord Jesus Christ at His coming? ²⁰ For you are our glory and joy.

3. Paul states that he was "taken away" from the believers in Thessalonica (verse 17). The Greek verb that he employs actually means "to make someone an orphan." Paul was anguished in having to be separated from the Thessalonians and longed to be reunited with them. What was the reason for Paul's prolonged separation from them (see verse 18)?

_____

_____

_____

_____

_____

_____

_____

_____

_____

_____

_____

4. The "crown" that Paul mentions (verse 19) likely refers to the laurel wreath, which was symbolic for victory and used as a prize for the winner of an athletic contest (see, for example, 1 Corinthians 9:24–27 and Philippians 3:12–14). What is the "victory" that Paul declares in this passage? Why does he have such pride in the believers (see verses 19–20)?

_____

_____

_____

_____

_____

_____

_____

_____

GOING DEEPER

The believers in Thessalonica were not the only followers of Christ who were experiencing persecution for their faith. The believers in Philippi, for example, were also facing many trials as a result of their acceptance of the gospel. In Paul's letter to that congregation, he urges the believers to embrace the opportunities that suffering brought them—including the opportunity to come together in unity and the opportunity to grow closer to Christ.

Striving and Suffering for Christ (Philippians 1:27–30)

27 Only let your conduct be worthy of the gospel of Christ, so that whether I come and see you or am absent, I may hear of your affairs, that you stand fast in one spirit, with one mind striving together for the faith of the gospel, 28 and not in any way terrified by your adversaries, which is to them a proof of perdition, but to you of salvation, and that from God. 29 For to you it has been granted on behalf of Christ, not only to believe in Him, but also to suffer for His sake, 30 having the same conflict which you saw in me and now hear is in me.

5. When Paul wrote this letter to the church at Philippi, he was in prison because of his devotion to Christ and to the gospel. Yet even in prison, Paul continued to proclaim the gospel and lead by example. How does Paul want the believers in Philippi to likewise respond to the persecution and suffering they were experiencing (see verses 27–28)?

_____

_____

_____

_____

_____

_____

_____

6. Many of the Philippians had converted from a pagan background that taught that happiness was the ultimate goal of religion. Paul wants them to understand what it _truly_ meant to live as a Christian. What "privilege" had the Philippian believers been granted because of their faith in Christ (see verses 29–30)?

_____

_____

_____

_____

_____

_____

_____

In his second letter to Timothy, Paul offers words of encouragement to _all_ who suffer for the cause of Christ. He points out that suffering is one of the marks of a godly life. For Paul, believers could, in many ways, gauge their godliness by their response to this suffering.

The Man of God and the Word of God (2 Timothy 3:10–17)

¹⁰ But you have carefully followed my doctrine, manner of life, purpose, faith, longsuffering, love, perseverance, ¹¹ persecutions, afflictions, which happened to me at Antioch, at Iconium, at Lystra—what persecutions I endured. And out of them all the Lord delivered me. ¹² Yes, and all who desire to live godly in Christ Jesus will suffer persecution. ¹³ But evil men and impostors will grow worse and worse, deceiving and being deceived. ¹⁴ But you must continue in the things which you have learned and been assured of, knowing from whom you have learned them, ¹⁵ and that from childhood you have known the Holy Scriptures, which are able to make you wise for salvation through faith which is in Christ Jesus.

¹⁶ All Scripture is given by inspiration of God, and is profitable for doctrine, for reproof, for correction, for instruction in righteousness, ¹⁷ that the man of God may be complete, thoroughly equipped for every good work.

---

7. What did Paul's persecutions and afflictions at Antioch, Iconium, and Lystra all have in common (see verses 10–11)?

_____

_____

_____

_____

_____

_____

_____

_____

_____

_____

_____

_____

8. Paul reminds Timothy that "all who desire to live godly in Christ Jesus will suffer persecution" (verse 12). This reflects Jesus' words to His followers: "If they persecuted Me, they will also persecute you" (John 15:20). What is the best way for believers to prepare for the inevitable persecution they will face (see 2 Timothy 3:14–17)?

_____

_____

_____

_____

_____

_____

REVIEWING THE STORY

As Paul continues to encourage the believers in Thessalonica, he recalls their conversion and the way that they had embraced the divine origin of the gospel. He compares the Thessalonian church favorably with the churches in Judea that had survived and thrived in the midst of persecution and suffering. Paul also refers to an unpleasant set of circumstances that led to his separation from the Thessalonians and emphasizes his desire to be reunited with them. He describes the believers in Thessalonica as his "glory and joy" (1 Thessalonians 2:20).

9. Why was Paul thankful for the believers in Thessalonica (see 1 Thessalonians 2:13)?

_____

_____

_____

_____

_____

10. How had the Judeans interfered with Paul's ministry (see 1 Thessalonians 2:15–16)?

_____

_____

_____

_____

_____

_____

_____

11. What did Paul reveal about the Judeans that must have given hope to the Thessalonians about their own oppressors (see 1 Thessalonians 2:16)?

_____

_____

_____

_____

_____

_____

_____

12. What did the Thessalonian believers mean to Paul (see 1 Thessalonians 2:19–20)?

_____

_____

_____

_____

_____

_____

_____

APPLYING THE MESSAGE

13. How did you first receive the "word of God" into your life?

_____

_____

_____

_____

_____

_____

_____

14. What are some ways that you have seen the enemy hinder your efforts for God?

_____

_____

_____

_____

_____

_____

_____

REFLECTING ON THE MEANING

In this section of Paul's letter, he offers a startling three-word explanation as to why he had been unable to return to Thessalonica: "Satan hindered us" (1 Thessalonians 2:18). The Greek word translated *hindered* is a military term that referred to the breaking up of bridges and roads to slow the invading army's progress. In spiritual terms, Satan gets in the way of God's work. He breaks up the paths of the gospel and tears down the bridges between people that make evangelism possible. The Bible reveals there are several strategies he employs to do this.

First, Satan can delay the answers to our prayers. In the book of Daniel, an angel explained to Daniel that Satan had delayed his prayers. "But the prince of the kingdom of Persia withstood me twenty-one days; and behold, Michael, one of the chief princes, came to help me, for I had been left alone there with the kings of Persia" (10:13). Daniel's prayer had been delayed *twenty-one* days because of spiritual conflict. Sometimes when we pray, we may wonder why there has been no answer. Something may be going on behind the scenes of which we are unaware. There could be a spiritual conflict hindering the answer to our prayers.

Second, Satan can deceive us in our walk with God. In the book of Acts, we read how Ananias and Sapphira lied to the church about donating all the proceeds from the sale of their land. Peter confronted Ananias with these words: "Ananias, why has Satan filled your heart to lie to the Holy Spirit and keep back part of the price of the land for yourself?" (5:3). Satan can fill our hearts to do evil if we are not on guard against his attacks.

Third, Satan can discourage us through affliction. In the book of Job, we read, "Satan went out from the presence of the LORD, and struck Job with painful boils from the sole of his foot to the crown of his head" (Job 2:7). Satan used this strategy in an attempt to cause the righteous Job to doubt God—and the enemy did so with God's permission. Satan always has to operate within the realm of God's control.

Fourth, Satan can derail our influence for God. The apostle Peter warned, "Be sober, be vigilant; because your adversary the devil walks about like a roaring lion, seeking whom he may devour" (1 Peter 5:8). Satan can take away any influence a person may have. If we are not careful, he can keep us from being effective servants of Almighty God.

In the words of Paul, the enemy will use these strategies "time and again" to hinder our effectiveness for Christ (1 Thessalonians 2:18). This is why we need to *pray* and *be prepared*. We need to pray and put on the whole armor of God so we can stand strong against our enemy (see Ephesians 6:10–20). As we do, he will flee from us (see James 4:7).

JOURNALING YOUR RESPONSE

In what area of your life have you experienced a spiritual attack that threatened to diminish your Christian influence?

LESSON *four*

GROWING UP
IN THE FAITH

1 Thessalonians 3:1–13

GETTING STARTED

What spiritual disciplines have helped you grow in your faith?

SETTING THE STAGE

Paul began his first letter to the Thessalonians by speaking about *salvation* and what it means to know the Lord. He continued by speaking about *ministry* and what it means to serve the Lord (see 1 Thessalonians 1–2). Now, as we come to 1 Thessalonians 3, Paul will speak about *sanctification* and what it means to grow in the Lord. His words in this section describe the essence of what it means to be a pastor—of what it means to help others to grow up in the Lord.

As we discovered in the last lesson, Paul had been pulled away from the believers in Thessalonica for reasons unknown to us. He explained the impact the separation had on him: "But we, brethren, having been taken away from you for a short time in presence, not in heart, endeavored more eagerly to see your face with great desire" (2:17). It is clear that Paul *wanted* to see them again, to make sure they were growing in their faith. But Satan had in some way hindered him from doing so.

As we will discover in this next section of Paul's letter, the apostle felt as though he had been orphaned from his friends. It must have been a time of great frustration for him. Were the believers still walking in the Lord? Were they weathering the storms of persecution? Were they able to stand the test as young believers? Fortunately, although Paul was not able to visit the believers himself, he was able to send his trusted colleague Timothy to visit them.

As Paul states, "Therefore, when we could no longer endure it, we thought it good to be left in Athens alone, and sent Timothy, our brother and minister of God, and our fellow laborer in the gospel of Christ, to establish you and encourage you concerning your faith" (1 Thessalonians 3:1–2). Timothy's visit to the church eased many of Paul's concerns. And it also caused him to express even greater thanksgiving for the believers' growth in the Lord.

EXPLORING THE TEXT

Concern for Their Faith (1 Thessalonians 3:1–8)

---

¹ Therefore, when we could no longer endure it, we thought it good to be left in Athens alone, ² and sent Timothy, our brother

and minister of God, and our fellow laborer in the gospel of Christ, to establish you and encourage you concerning your faith, ³ that no one should be shaken by these afflictions; for you yourselves know that we are appointed to this. ⁴ For, in fact, we told you before when we were with you that we would suffer tribulation, just as it happened, and you know. ⁵ For this reason, when I could no longer endure it, I sent to know your faith, lest by some means the tempter had tempted you, and our labor might be in vain.

⁶ But now that Timothy has come to us from you, and brought us good news of your faith and love, and that you always have good remembrance of us, greatly desiring to see us, as we also to see you—⁷ therefore, brethren, in all our affliction and distress we were comforted concerning you by your faith. ⁸ For now we live, if you stand fast in the Lord.

---

1. As Luke reports, Paul and his companions had been suddenly driven out of the city of Thessalonica and were unable to stay and continue to disciple the new converts (see Acts 17:1–9). Paul knew that the new believers were being "shaken by . . . afflictions" (1 Thessalonians 3:3). How does he express his concern for them (see verses 1–5)?

2. Paul states twice that he could no longer "endure it" when it came to knowing whether the believers were growing in their faith (verses 1, 5). So, he sent his coworker Timothy to find out what was happening in the church. Timothy reported that the believers were not only continuing in "faith and love" (verse 6) but also remembering Paul and his companions with fondness. What impact did Timothy's update have on Paul during his own time of affliction and distress (see verses 6–8)?

_____

_____

_____

_____

_____

_____

_____

_____

Encouraged by Timothy (1 Thessalonians 3:9–13)

⁹ For what thanks can we render to God for you, for all the joy with which we rejoice for your sake before our God, ¹⁰ night and day praying exceedingly that we may see your face and perfect what is lacking in your faith?

¹¹ Now may our God and Father Himself, and our Lord Jesus Christ, direct our way to you. ¹² And may the Lord make you increase and abound in love to one another and to all, just as we do to you, ¹³ so that He may establish your hearts blameless in holiness before our God and Father at the coming of our Lord Jesus Christ with all His saints.

3. Paul's use of the term "night and day" should likely be taken figuratively rather than literally (verse 10). Paul is basically describing how frequently he had been lifting up his brothers and sisters in

Thessalonica in his prayers. What were the two key requests that Paul maintained in his continual prayers for the believers (see verses 9–10)?

_____

_____

_____

_____

_____

_____

4. Paul's prayers were answered, and he was able to return to Thessalonica some five years after he wrote these verses (see Acts 19:21; 20:1; 1 Corinthians 16:5; 2 Corinthians 2:13). What does Paul say he wants God to do for the believers in his absence? How does he desire the believers to grow in their faith and their example to others (see verses 11–12)?

_____

_____

_____

_____

_____

_____

GOING DEEPER

Paul was not the only early church leader who recognized the importance and necessity of persecution in the life of a believer. Both Peter and James also explained to their readers that trials are just to be expected. As the following passages relate, Peter urged his readers to "rejoice" when they experienced trials, for it was evidence that the Spirit of God rested on them. James asked his readers to "count it all joy" when they endured trials, for it enabled them to develop patience—which is one of the most valuable tools in the Christian's toolbox.

Suffering for God's Glory (1 Peter 4:12–19)

¹² Beloved, do not think it strange concerning the fiery trial which is to try you, as though some strange thing happened to you; ¹³ but rejoice to the extent that you partake of Christ's sufferings, that when His glory is revealed, you may also be glad with exceeding joy. ¹⁴ If you are reproached for the name of Christ, blessed are you, for the Spirit of glory and of God rests upon you. On their part He is blasphemed, but on your part He is glorified. ¹⁵ But let none of you suffer as a murderer, a thief, an evildoer, or as a busybody in other people's matters. ¹⁶ Yet if anyone suffers as a Christian, let him not be ashamed, but let him glorify God in this matter.

¹⁷ For the time has come for judgment to begin at the house of God; and if it begins with us first, what will be the end of those who do not obey the gospel of God? ¹⁸ Now

"If the righteous one is scarcely saved,
Where will the ungodly and the sinner appear?"

¹⁹ Therefore let those who suffer according to the will of God commit their souls to Him in doing good, as to a faithful Creator.

5. Peter addresses his readers with fatherly affection as he seeks to change their perspective on human suffering. Although the world responds to suffering with shock and disapproval, Christians are to view it as a means to reveal their genuine faith. What does Peter say is the proper response for a Christian who experiences suffering (see verses 12–16)?

6. Peter quotes Proverbs 11:31 to describe the Lord's judgment on the ungodly: "If the righteous will be recompensed on the earth, how much more the ungodly and the sinner." In other words, God's judgment will be indescribable for those who reject Jesus as their Lord. How would this have encouraged his readers to stay the course in their faith? How are believers called to live in light of the reality of God's judgment (see verses 17–19)?

_____

_____

_____

_____

_____

_____

_____

_____

_____

Profiting from Trials (James 1:2–8)

² My brethren, count it all joy when you fall into various trials, ³ knowing that the testing of your faith produces patience. ⁴ But let patience have its perfect work, that you may be perfect and complete, lacking nothing. ⁵ If any of you lacks wisdom, let him ask of God, who gives to all liberally and without reproach, and it will be given to him. ⁶ But let him ask in faith, with no doubting, for he who doubts is like a wave of the sea driven and tossed by the wind. ⁷ For let not that man suppose that he will receive anything from the Lord; ⁸ he is a double-minded man, unstable in all his ways.

7. James's readers would have been familiar with certain passages from the Old Testament that speak of people's hearts being tested in a furnace (see, for example, Proverbs 17:3 and Isaiah 48:10–11). In those contexts, the fire of testing refers to trials and afflictions that serve to strengthen the faith of God's people. How does James say these trials should affect the character of a believer in Christ (see James 1:2–4)?

_____

_____

_____

_____

_____

_____

8. James uses the word *wisdom* in verse 5 to describe an understanding of who God is and how He wants His people to live and act in this world. How does doubt hinder us from receiving the wisdom we need to navigate trials and suffering in life (see verses 5–8)?

_____

_____

_____

_____

_____

_____

_____

REVIEWING THE STORY

Like an anxious parent, Paul recounts his suspense at not knowing the fate of his spiritual children in Thessalonica. He had been separated from them at a critical point in their spiritual development, and he wanted to know the impact of that separation and how they had fared in the midst of their suffering. The apostle was so eager for news from the Thessalonians that he sent Timothy to visit them while he remained alone back in the city of Athens. The news that Timothy brought back had overjoyed Paul. He now expresses his fervent desire to be reunited with the Thessalonians so he can help them perfect their already impressive faith.

9. What warning had Paul issued to the Thessalonian believers that proved to be prophetic (see 1 Thessalonians 3:4)?

_____

_____

_____

_____

_____

10. What was Paul's worst fear concerning the new believers in Thessalonica (see 1 Thessalonians 3:5)?

_____

_____

_____

_____

_____

11. How would you describe Paul's reaction to the news that he received about the believers in Thessalonica (see 1 Thessalonians 3:9–10)?

_____

_____

_____

_____

12. What did Paul pray would happen in the relationships of the new believers in Thessalonica (see 1 Thessalonians 3:11–12)?

_____

_____

_____

_____

_____

_____

APPLYING THE MESSAGE

13. How have your brothers and sisters in Christ helped to _establish_ you in your faith?

_____

_____

_____

_____

_____

_____

14. How have your brothers and sisters in Christ _encouraged_ you concerning your faith?

_____

_____

_____

_____

_____

_____

_____

REFLECTING ON THE MEANING

The apostle Paul writes the following words to the new believers in Thessalonica: "For what thanks can we render to God for you, for all the joy with which we rejoice for your sake before our God, night and day praying exceedingly that we may see your faith and perfect what is lacking in your faith" (1 Thessalonians 3:9–10). Following Paul's example, there are several ways that we are to pray for new Christians.

First, we are to pray thankfully. As Paul writes, "For what thanks can we render to God for you" (verse 9). Before the apostle even begins to pray for the Thessalonians believers, he gives thanks for them and their faith. Likewise, we should start our prayers by thanking God for the fact that people have come to the faith.

Second, we are to pray joyfully. Paul writes, "For all the joy with which we rejoice for your sake before God" (verse 9). Paul can hardly contain his excitement and joy as he talks about the Thessalonian believers. Likewise, we should be excited and joyful at what God will accomplish in and through new believers in our world. We should rejoice in knowing that God has recruited fellow workers for the gospel.

Third, we are to pray continually. Paul states that he is praying for the believers "night and day" (verse 10). Morning and evening—while he was working on his tents, or walking in the streets, or conducting his other affairs—his prayers were flowing out of his concern and love for these new believers. They were seldom out of his thoughts, and wherever he went, he prayed for them. We should be praying the same way.

Fourth, we are to pray fervently. Paul states that he not only prays night and day for the believers but also that he prays "exceedingly" for them (verse 10). This suggests an intense agonizing over the fate of new believers. It mattered deeply to Paul that the Thessalonians would continue to grow in their faith and stand strong in the midst of trials and suffering. We cannot just *pray* for new believers—we must pray earnestly and intensely for them.

Paul's words reveal that when we lead another person to faith in Christ, we can't just stop there. Rather, we must follow Paul's example of praying thankfully, joyfully, continually, and fervently for our new brother or sister in the faith.

JOURNALING YOUR RESPONSE

How will you pray today for the new believers in your circle of acquaintances?

THE CALL TO A HOLY LIFE

1 Thessalonians 4:1–18

GETTING STARTED

What does it mean to be holy? How would you describe what it means to lead a holy life?

_____

_____

_____

_____

_____

_____

_____

_____

_____

_____

_____

_____

SETTING THE STAGE

Paul closes the previous chapter of his letter with the words, "May [the Lord] establish your hearts blameless in holiness before our God and Father at the coming of our Lord Jesus Christ with all His saints" (1 Thessalonians 3:13). Now, in 1 Thessalonians 4, he expands on this goal that he has for the believers. He is satisfied with their faith and doctrine, but he wants to know exactly *what* that faith and doctrine were producing in their lives.

When we study the structure of Paul's letters, we discover that he typically spends the first half laying a doctrinal foundation for his readers, and the second half explaining how that doctrinal foundation should play out in their lives. Up to this point in his letter, Paul has been laying a doctrinal foundation for holiness for the believers in Thessalonica. Now, he is going to help them understand what it actually means to *lead* a holy life.

Specifically, Paul is going to expound on the concept of *sanctification*, which is the process of becoming holy. The believers had already experienced what we might call *positional* sanctification. It took place when they accepted Jesus as their Savior and received salvation. Paul now wants them to experience *progressive* sanctification. He wants them to grow in their faith "more and more" (verse 1) so they could continue to become more like Christ. Ultimately, he desires for them to obtain what we might call *perfect* sanctification, which would take place when they reached heaven and the process of their holiness was complete.

As we look at Paul's words, we find that sanctification has *past, present,* and *future* elements. It is possible for us to say, "I *was* saved, I am *being* saved, and I *will be* saved." In many ways, sanctification is the process of becoming in practice what we already are in perfection. Every day, we are to live according to what we already are in heaven.

EXPLORING THE TEXT

A Plea for Purity (1 Thessalonians 4:1–8)

> [1] Finally then, brethren, we urge and exhort in the Lord Jesus that you should abound more and more, just as you received from us how you ought to walk and to please God; [2] for you know what commandments we gave you through the Lord Jesus.

³ For this is the will of God, your sanctification: that you should abstain from sexual immorality; ⁴ that each of you should know how to possess his own vessel in sanctification and honor, ⁵ not in passion of lust, like the Gentiles who do not know God; ⁶ that no one should take advantage of and defraud his brother in this matter, because the Lord is the avenger of all such, as we also forewarned you and testified. ⁷ For God did not call us to uncleanness, but in holiness. ⁸ Therefore he who rejects this does not reject man, but God, who has also given us His Holy Spirit.

---

1. Paul reminds the believers of the teachings he delivered when he was with them. Rather than demanding certain behavioral changes from them at this point, he instead affirms them and urges them forward in their faith. What does Paul desire the believers to continue doing? According to Paul, what is God's ultimate will for them (see verses 1–3)?

_____

_____

_____

_____

_____

_____

_____

_____

_____

_____

2. Christians are to be holy in all areas of their lives, but in these verses Paul focuses on sexual morality. In the pagan culture in Thessalonica, sexual immorality was not only practiced but also tolerated. So, as a new community of believers, the Thessalonian church needed spiritual guidance in this area. What teaching does Paul give the believers regarding their need to maintain sexual purity and avoid sexual immorality (see verses 3–8)?

_____

_____

_____

_____

_____

A Brotherly and Orderly Life (1 Thessalonians 4:9–18)

9 But concerning brotherly love you have no need that I should write to you, for you yourselves are taught by God to love one another; 10 and indeed you do so toward all the brethren who are in all Macedonia. But we urge you, brethren, that you increase more and more; 11 that you also aspire to lead a quiet life, to mind your own business, and to work with your own hands, as we commanded you, 12 that you may walk properly toward those who are outside, and that you may lack nothing.

13 But I do not want you to be ignorant, brethren, concerning those who have fallen asleep, lest you sorrow as others who have no hope. 14 For if we believe that Jesus died and rose again, even so God will bring with Him those who sleep in Jesus.

15 For this we say to you by the word of the Lord, that we who are alive and remain until the coming of the Lord will by no means precede those who are asleep. 16 For the Lord Himself will descend from heaven with a shout, with the voice of an archangel, and with the trumpet of God. And the dead in Christ will rise first. 17 Then we who are alive and remain shall be caught up together with them in the clouds to meet the Lord in the air. And thus we shall always be with the Lord. 18 Therefore comfort one another with these words.

3. Paul wanted to establish a boundary between the Thessalonian church and the pagan culture surrounding them—whom he calls "those who are outside" (verse 12). He does this by addressing behaviors that should be evident in the lives of the believers. According to Paul, how should the Thessalonians conduct their lives in a way that reveals the brotherly love that should exist among believers (see verses 9–12)?

_____

_____

_____

_____

4. Paul touches on the topic of the Rapture in this passage. How does he describe the events that will take place upon Christ's return to this world (see verses 16–17)?

_____

_____

_____

_____

_____

GOING DEEPER

In Paul's first letter to believers in the city of Corinth, he provides a compelling reason as to why Christians are to pursue a holy life. Paul describes the believers' bodies as the "temple" of the Holy Spirit, who actively dwells within them. Just as they would never defile a physical temple, so they are not to defile their spiritual temple through sexual immorality. Rather, they are to pursue holiness to reflect the holiness of the One who resides within them.

Glorify God in Body and Spirit (1 Corinthians 6:12–20)

¹² All things are lawful for me, but all things are not helpful. All things are lawful for me, but I will not be brought under the power of any. ¹³ Foods for the stomach and the stomach for foods, but God will destroy both it and them. Now the body is not for sexual immorality but for the Lord, and the Lord for the body. ¹⁴ And God both raised up the Lord and will also raise us up by His power.

¹⁵ Do you not know that your bodies are members of Christ? Shall I then take the members of Christ and make them members of a harlot? Certainly not! ¹⁶ Or do you not know that he who is joined to a harlot is one body with her? For "the two," He says, "shall become one flesh." ¹⁷ But he who is joined to the Lord is one spirit with Him.

¹⁸ Flee sexual immorality. Every sin that a man does is outside the body, but he who commits sexual immorality sins against his own body. ¹⁹ Or do you not know that your body is the temple of the Holy Spirit who is in you, whom you have from God, and you are not your own? ²⁰ For you were bought at a price; therefore glorify God in your body and in your spirit, which are God's.

---

5. Some of the Christians in Corinth believed their faith in Christ gave them the freedom to set their own standards for how they used their bodies and what they put into them. Paul does not dispute this belief, but he does warn them of getting caught up in behaviors that are not helpful and that lead to enslavement to sin rather than freedom. What is Paul's teaching to the believers about how they should regard and use their bodies (see verses 12–17)?

_____

_____

_____

_____

6. Paul directly addresses the issue of sexual immorality with the Corinthian believers, who lived in a culture that widely accepted ritual prostitution. He warns them of the dangers of becoming enslaved by the power of immorality and urges them to flee from this behavior. He notes that sexual sin, unlike other sins that are committed outside the body, involves the *entire* person. With this in mind, what reasoning does Paul provide to convince the Corinthian believers of the sinfulness of sexual immorality (see verses 18–20)?

_____

_____

_____

_____

_____

_____

_____

Peter also writes to believers about the importance of pursuing a godly life. In the following passage, he calls on his readers to set aside the evil desires that had characterized their lives before they found Jesus. He implores them instead to model the holiness of Christ.

Leading a Holy Life (1 Peter 1:13–21)

13 Therefore gird up the loins of your mind, be sober, and rest your hope fully upon the grace that is to be brought to you at the revelation of Jesus Christ; 14 as obedient children, not conforming yourselves to the former lusts, as in your ignorance; 15 but as He who called you is holy, you also be holy in all your conduct, 16 because it is written, "Be holy, for I am holy."

17 And if you call on the Father, who without partiality judges according to each one's work, conduct yourselves throughout the time of your stay here in fear; 18 knowing that you were not redeemed

with corruptible things, like silver or gold, from your aimless conduct received by tradition from your fathers, ¹⁹ but with the precious blood of Christ, as of a lamb without blemish and without spot. ²⁰ He indeed was foreordained before the foundation of the world, but was manifest in these last times for you ²¹ who through Him believe in God, who raised Him from the dead and gave Him glory, so that your faith and hope are in God.

---

7. Peter instructs his readers to "gird up the loins" of their minds (verse 13). In his day, people would wear a belt around their waist so their garments would not trip them up or constrict movement. In the same way, believers are to not be tripped up or encumbered by their former ways of life. What does Peter say they are to pursue (see verses 13–16)?

_____

_____

_____

_____

_____

8. Peter stresses that believers in Christ have not been redeemed with the riches of this world—with "corruptible things, like silver or gold" (verse 18). What was the cost of their redemption? How should this affect the way they conduct themselves (see verses 17–19)?

_____

_____

_____

_____

_____

REVIEWING THE STORY

Paul urges the Thessalonians to follow God's commandments and increase in personal holiness. He states that God's will is for them to be *sanctified* and abstain from sexual immorality. He implores them to not defraud their fellow brothers and sisters in Christ in this matter, for the one who rejects this teaching rejects not *man* but actually *God*. Paul commands them to seek to lead a quiet life, to mind their own business, and to work diligently. He concludes with an assurance that their loved ones in the faith who have died have not missed the resurrection. He explains the events that will transpire at Jesus' second coming, when the dead in Christ will first rise up, followed by the living, and all will meet Christ in the Rapture.

9. What did Paul encourage the believers to do as it relates to growing in personal holiness (see 1 Thessalonians 4:1)?

_____

_____

_____

_____

_____

10. What has God given believers to help in their pursuit of holiness (see 1 Thessalonians 4:8)?

_____

_____

_____

_____

_____

_____

11. Why did Paul not need to instruct the Thessalonian believers about brotherly love (see 1 Thessalonians 4:9–10)?

_____

_____

_____

_____

_____

12. What did Paul want the Thessalonian believers to do with the information he had previously related about the return of Christ (see 1 Thessalonians 4:18)?

_____

_____

_____

_____

_____

APPLYING THE MESSAGE

13. What are some of the challenges that believers face today when it comes to pursuing personal holiness?

_____

_____

_____

_____

_____

14. What wisdom can you draw from Paul's words to the Thessalonians that can help you in your pursuit of holiness?

_____

_____

_____

_____

_____

REFLECTING ON THE MEANING

Paul says in this section of his letter that sanctification is the will of God for us (see 1 Thessalonians 4:3), and that God has called us to pursue a life of holiness (see verse 7). In other words, we are to lead a *holy* life! But what does this actually mean? What standards determine whether or not we are conducting ourselves in a holy manner?

First, a holy life is a life of progress with God. Paul writes, "We urge and exhort . . . that you should abound more and more" (verse 1). There is no plateau in the Christian life. When we think we've arrived at a certain place of understanding, we quickly realize we have more to know. Holiness is a dynamic, progressive walk with God.

Second, a holy life is a life of purity. Paul states, "This is the will of God . . . that you should abstain from sexual immorality" (verse 3). If we want God to bless us, we must govern ourselves as He demands. We must encourage each other to pursue holiness. We must ask God to help us abstain from sexual immorality as we allow the Holy Spirit to have control over our bodies. Each of us must honor God by treating our body with respect and by keeping it pure.

Third, a holy life is a powerfully transformed life. Paul warns, "He who rejects this [teaching] does not reject man, but God, who has also given us His Holy Spirit" (verse 8). Our outward lives should reflect the inward change we have experienced. If we are truly born again, the world should see the difference in us. This means not only demonstrating our conviction to lead a *pure* life but also to lead a life of *humility* and *honesty*. As we do this, we will truly begin to reflect God's holiness to the world around us.

JOURNALING YOUR RESPONSE

What do you want people to see when they look at your life?

THE BELIEVER AND THE TRIBULATION

1 Thessalonians 5:1–11

GETTING STARTED

What thoughts come to mind when you think of the return of Christ?

_____

_____

_____

_____

_____

_____

_____

_____

_____

_____

_____

_____

_____

_____

_____

_____

_____

_____

_____

_____

SETTING THE STAGE

Paul closed the previous chapter of his letter by describing the next event on the church's prophetic calendar: the Rapture. On that day, Jesus will descend in the clouds and bring the church to Himself. The dead in Christ will rise first, followed by those who are alive at His appearing (see 1 Thessalonians 4:15–17). The Rapture of the church could happen at any moment—even while you are reading this Bible study!

The Rapture results in two events. First, it will bring to a conclusion the age of grace, when we have the opportunity to receive Christ here on earth. Second, it will usher in the Tribulation period. This is a seven-year period when the Holy Spirit—and the church—is removed from the earth and great judgments are unleashed. The last three-and-a-half years are known as the Great Tribulation. During this time, plagues and destruction will be intensified before the ultimate battle—the battle of Armageddon.

The Rapture and Tribulation begin a period the Old Testament prophets called "the day of the Lord"—which Paul will now address in his letter to the Thessalonians. This is a matter for believers in Christ to take seriously and to treat as urgent. We must tell others of the hope they can have in Christ, for when the Rapture occurs, all godly influence in the world will disappear. There will be no restraining influence left on the earth.

As Paul writes, "the day of the Lord so comes as a thief in the night" (1 Thessalonians 5:2). For this reason, we need to be prepared at all times for that day to arrive. And we also need to bring as many people as we can into God's kingdom to escape this coming judgment.

EXPLORING THE TEXT

The Day of the Lord (1 Thessalonians 5:1–5)

¹ But concerning the times and the seasons, brethren, you have no need that I should write to you. ² For you yourselves know perfectly that the day of the Lord so comes as a thief in the night. ³ For when

they say, "Peace and safety!" then sudden destruction comes upon them, as labor pains upon a pregnant woman. And they shall not escape. [4] But you, brethren, are not in darkness, so that this Day should overtake you as a thief. [5] You are all sons of light and sons of the day. We are not of the night nor of darkness.

---

1. While there is no consensus among biblical scholars as to the original context of the phrase "peace and safety" (verse 3), it accurately describes the complacency of people living in the world without a thought about the future. What impact will the day of the Lord have on people's false sense of peace and safety (see verses 2–3)?

_____

_____

_____

_____

_____

_____

2. In this passage, Paul refers to unbelievers as "they" (verse 3) and to believers in Christ as "we" and the "brethren" (verses 4–5). How will the believers' experience of the day of the Lord differ from the unbelievers' experience (see verses 3–5)?

_____

_____

_____

_____

_____

_____

_____

_____

Keep Watch and Stay Sober (1 Thessalonians 5:6–11)

⁶ Therefore let us not sleep, as others do, but let us watch and be sober. ⁷ For those who sleep, sleep at night, and those who get drunk are drunk at night. ⁸ But let us who are of the day be sober, putting on the breastplate of faith and love, and as a helmet the hope of salvation. ⁹ For God did not appoint us to wrath, but to obtain salvation through our Lord Jesus Christ, ¹⁰ who died for us, that whether we wake or sleep, we should live together with Him.

¹¹ Therefore comfort each other and edify one another, just as you also are doing.

3. Paul is clear that ignoring spiritual matters is not an option for those who follow Christ. How should believers live in a way that reveals their active attention to the coming day of the Lord (see verses 6–8)?

_____

_____

_____

_____

_____

_____

_____

_____

_____

_____

4. Paul reassures the Thessalonian believers their salvation is secure because Jesus died to "obtain salvation" for them (verse 9). They therefore had no reason to worry about being subjected to the wrath to come on the day of the Lord. Given this, how are believers called to respond to the hope they have in their salvation (see verses 9–11)?

_____

_____

_____

_____

_____

_____

_____

_____

_____

_____

_____

_____

GOING DEEPER

God proclaimed many warnings to His people about the coming day of the Lord long before He sent His Son into the world to provide a means of salvation from it. Centuries before Jesus' birth, the Old Testament prophet Zephaniah used words such as *wrath*, *distress*, *devastation*, *desolation*, and *darkness* to describe what awaits those who reject God's salvation.

The Great Day of the Lord (Zephaniah 1:14–18)

14 The great day of the LORD is near;
It is near and hastens quickly.
The noise of the day of the LORD is bitter;
There the mighty men shall cry out.
15 That day is a day of wrath,
A day of trouble and distress,
A day of devastation and desolation,
A day of darkness and gloominess,
A day of clouds and thick darkness,

^{16} A day of trumpet and alarm
Against the fortified cities
And against the high towers.

^{17} "I will bring distress upon men,
And they shall walk like blind men,
Because they have sinned against the LORD;
Their blood shall be poured out like dust,
And their flesh like refuse."

^{18} Neither their silver nor their gold
Shall be able to deliver them
In the day of the LORD's wrath;
But the whole land shall be devoured
By the fire of His jealousy,
For He will make speedy riddance
Of all those who dwell in the land.

---

5. The Israelites expected the day of the Lord to be one of victory and celebration—a day when God would pour out His wrath on Israel's enemies. Zephaniah, however, paints a much darker picture for Israel. On the day of the Lord, God will unleash His judgment on all who "have sinned against the LORD" (verse 17)—including the people of Israel. In these verses, how does the prophet describe this day of judgment (see verses 14–16)?

_____

_____

_____

_____

_____

_____

6. A holy God responds to sin with anger and judgment. His anger is due to His "jealousy" (verse 18). When God is described as jealous, it means He alone is worthy of honor, and He alone should be given our obedience and worship. How does Zephaniah describe the effects of God unleashing His jealous wrath on those who refuse to repent (see verses 17–18)?

_____

_____

_____

_____

_____

_____

_____

_____

_____

God also proclaimed warnings to His people about the coming day of the Lord after Jesus came into the world. In the book of Revelation, the Lord revealed vivid details to the apostle John about Jesus' second coming. This event, which will feature Christ on a white horse, will bring the seven-year period of Tribulation to a close and usher in Christ's kingdom on earth.

Christ on a White Horse (Revelation 19:11–16)

11 Now I saw heaven opened, and behold, a white horse. And He who sat on him was called Faithful and True, and in righteousness He judges and makes war. 12 His eyes were like a flame of fire, and on His head were many crowns. He had a name written that no one knew except Himself. 13 He was clothed with a robe dipped in blood, and His name is called The Word of God. 14 And the armies in heaven, clothed in fine linen, white and clean, followed Him on white horses. 15 Now out of His mouth goes a sharp sword, that with it He should strike the nations. And He Himself will rule them with a rod of iron. He Himself treads

the winepress of the fierceness and wrath of Almighty God. [16] And He has on His robe and on His thigh a name written:

KING OF KINGS AND
LORD OF LORDS.

---

7. John describes Jesus' coming in language that is reminiscent of how a Roman emperor would have returned from a significant victory. A triumphant emperor would have worn a golden crown, with an ornately decorated white tunic, and entered the city on a chariot drawn by white horses. How is Jesus described in these verses? Why is He able to pronounce ultimate judgment on the world (see verses 11–16)?

_____

_____

_____

_____

_____

_____

8. Unlike a Roman emperor, who would have unleashed his army and his weapons on his enemies to defeat them, Jesus' only weapons of judgment include His own blood and the sword of God's Word (see verses 13, 15). How will Jesus pronounce and carry out judgment on the nations—the people who refused to worship Him as Lord (see verses 11, 15)?

_____

_____

_____

_____

REVIEWING THE STORY

Paul reminds the believers in Thessalonica that the day of the Lord is imminent—it can happen at any moment like the coming of a "thief in the night" (1 Thessalonians 5:2). The believers cannot predict when it will occur, but they can prepare for it. Paul emphasizes that he is not trying to make the Thessalonian believers uneasy with his teachings. Instead, he wants them to find comfort concerning their own future and encouragement to help others escape God's wrath.

9. What does Paul assure the Thessalonian believers would not happen because they were not living in darkness (see 1 Thessalonians 5:4)?

_____

_____

_____

_____

10. What were the believers to do since they were "sons of the day" and "not of the night" (see 1 Thessalonians 5:5–6)?

_____

_____

_____

_____

11. What promise does Paul make to the Thesalonians—and to us—regarding the coming day of the Lord (see 1 Thessalonians 5:9–10)?

_____

_____

_____

_____

12. What response does Paul want the Thessalonians to have when they considered the coming day of the Lord (see 1 Thessalonians 5:11)?

_____

_____

_____

_____

_____

APPLYING THE MESSAGE

13. How does your understanding of the day of the Lord affect the urgency you feel to share your faith with others?

_____

_____

_____

_____

_____

14. What can you do to lovingly warn your unbelieving loved ones, acquaintances, neighbors, and coworkers about God's righteous judgment during the Tribulation?

_____

_____

_____

_____

_____

REFLECTING ON THE MEANING

The Bible reveals that God has planned a time of judgment for those who reject Him—what the authors of Scripture call "the day of the Lord." This knowledge should inspire each of us to be busy in every way possible to bring people to Jesus Christ. So, today, the challenge for you is to find *one person* in your world who does not know the Lord, and then do two things: (1) invest some time in that person, and (2) invite that person to church to hear the gospel.

The apostle Paul had clearly *invested* a great amount of time in the believers in Thessalonica—encouraging them, admonishing them, praying for them, and urging them to continue to grow in holiness. He had also issued an *invitation* to them, calling them to participate in the local community that would represent the body of Christ. In the same way, you are called to *invest* in others and *invite* them into the community of faith.

Now, as you invest your time in that person, you may find that you are not able to answer all of his or her questions. You may not be prepared to explain all the claims made about Christ. But you can *invite* the person to church—and then watch what God can accomplish through that simple invitation. It may be the trigger that brings the person into a relationship with Christ. It may be the thing that earns you a heartfelt "thank you for bringing me to hear the gospel" from the person as the two of you ascend to meet Jesus in the air.

It is easy for us as believers to get comfortable in church. We enjoy the music, the preaching, and the fellowship . . . without it even dawning on us that God has also given us a mission in the world. We have already been found! What we need to do is find the people who *haven't* been found yet and share with them what God has done for us.

Remember, God has a wonderful plan for those who believe in Him and put their faith in Christ. If you know that you will be with Christ at the Rapture, and in heaven during the day of the Lord, pray that God will lead you to at least one other person who needs that same comfort and assurance.

JOURNALING YOUR RESPONSE

How will you lay the groundwork today for inviting an unbeliever to church?

ANTICIPATING JESUS' RETURN

1 Thessalonians 5:12–28

GETTING STARTED

What are some ways that you seek to maintain a spirit of thankfulness?

_____

_____

_____

_____

_____

_____

_____

_____

_____

_____

_____

_____

_____

_____

_____

_____

_____

_____

_____

_____

_____

SETTING THE STAGE

As Paul wraps up his first letter to the believers in Thessalonica, he seems to be reminded of all the things he still needs to tell them before he signs off. At the top of that list is the logical conclusion to the questions that he has answered for them. Remember, he has discussed the Rapture—the next event on the prophetic calendar—when all believers (along with the Holy Spirit within them) will be removed from the earth. He has talked about the day of the Lord and the horrific events of the Tribulation, which will occur on earth while believers are in heaven.

But before Paul ends his correspondence, he wants the believers to know how they should live in the meantime, in light of the fact that Jesus is coming back. Some of the Thessalonian believers had convinced themselves and others that because Jesus' return was imminent, they no longer needed to work. In effect, they had dropped out of society to wait for His coming. Paul corrects their misunderstanding and encourages them—and us—to work wisely and diligently as we anticipate the return of Christ.

Paul understood a failure to do this would lead to disunity in the body of Christ—which is a serious issue, as the body of Christ is the source of believers' power to confront the enemy's attacks. It would give people outside the church a reason to question their integrity. So instead, he urges the Thessalonians—and us—to accept our responsibilities as followers of Christ: "be at peace among yourselves . . . always pursue what is good . . . rejoice always, pray without ceasing, in everything give thanks" (1 Thessalonians 5:13, 15, 16–18). As we do these things, we serve as a beacon of light, and our witness will draw others into the family of God.

EXPLORING THE TEXT

Closing Exhortations (1 Thessalonians 5:12–22)

> [12] And we urge you, brethren, to recognize those who labor among you, and are over you in the Lord and admonish you, [13] and to

esteem them very highly in love for their work's sake. Be at peace among yourselves.

^{14} Now we exhort you, brethren, warn those who are unruly, comfort the fainthearted, uphold the weak, be patient with all. ^{15} See that no one renders evil for evil to anyone, but always pursue what is good both for yourselves and for all.

^{16} Rejoice always, ^{17} pray without ceasing, ^{18} in everything give thanks; for this is the will of God in Christ Jesus for you.

^{19} Do not quench the Spirit. ^{20} Do not despise prophecies. ^{21} Test all things; hold fast what is good. ^{22} Abstain from every form of evil.

---

1. Paul here is addressing a community of believers rather than specific individuals. He urges *all* believers to not only respect those whom God has placed as leaders in their church but also to encourage those who struggle with spiritual weakness in their midst. Based on this passage, what responsibilities does a congregation have to care for their leaders and members who are in need of encouragement (see verses 12–15)?

_____

_____

_____

_____

_____

_____

_____

_____

2. Earlier in Paul's letter, he reminded the Thessalonians of the "joy of the Holy Spirit" they each possessed (1:6). The Holy Spirit enabled them to maintain an attitude of joy in all circumstances (see 1 Thessalonians 5:16). What other actions and attitudes—besides rejoicing—should believers practice in order to fulfill God's will and follow the Holy Spirit's leading in their lives (see verses 16–22)?

_____

_____

_____

_____

_____

_____

_____

_____

_____

_____

_____

_____

_____

_____

Blessing and Admonition (1 Thessalonians 5:23–28)

23 Now may the God of peace Himself sanctify you completely; and may your whole spirit, soul, and body be preserved blameless at the coming of our Lord Jesus Christ. 24 He who calls you is faithful, who also will do it.

25 Brethren, pray for us.

26 Greet all the brethren with a holy kiss.

27 I charge you by the Lord that this epistle be read to all the holy brethren.

28 The grace of our Lord Jesus Christ be with you. Amen.

3. The word *sanctify* that Paul uses in verse 23 refers to the process that believers go through to become holy. According to Paul, who is responsible for producing holiness in our lives? When is the process of sanctification complete (see verses 23–24)?

_____

_____

_____

_____

_____

4. Paul closes with a command for the church to read his letter (see verse 27). Most people at the time were illiterate, so someone would have read the letter out loud to the community. How is Paul's tone different in verse 27 from his tone in verses 25–26? What does his choice of words communicate about the importance of reading his letter?

_____

_____

_____

_____

_____

_____

Going Deeper

Paul was not the only leader in the early church to plead for believers to live at peace with one another. In James' epistle, he also urges followers of Christ to pursue unity. Both men understood the indomitable strength that a united body of Christ possessed in the world. They also understood the damage caused when believers couldn't live at peace among themselves. James points out that our own selfish desires lead to strife with our Christian brothers and sisters. Instead, we need to humbly submit to God and leave the judging of others to Him.

Pride Promotes Strife (James 4:1–6)

¹ Where do wars and fights come from among you? Do they not come from your desires for pleasure that war in your members? ² You lust and do not have. You murder and covet and cannot obtain. You fight and war. Yet you do not have because you do not ask. ³ You ask and do not receive, because you ask amiss, that you may spend it on your pleasures. ⁴ Adulterers and adulteresses! Do you not know that friendship with the world is enmity with God? Whoever therefore wants to be a friend of the world makes himself an enemy of God. ⁵ Or do you think that the Scripture says in vain, "The Spirit who dwells in us yearns jealously"?

⁶ But He gives more grace. Therefore He says:

"God resists the proud,
But gives grace to the humble."

---

5. James addresses his letter to a church struggling with disunity and internal conflict. He calls the believers "adulterers and adulteresses"— an accusation used both by the Old Testament prophets and by Jesus to describe people who are unfaithful to God (see Jeremiah 5:7; Hosea 1:2–3; Matthew 12:39; 16:4; Mark 8:38). What unfaithful, "adulterous" behavior among believers does James point out in these verses (see James 4:1–4)?

_____

_____

_____

_____

_____

_____

_____

6. James describes the Holy Spirit as one who "yearns jealously" in the life of a believer (verse 5). God is rightly jealous for His bride—the church—to remain faithful to Him and continue in a covenant relationship with Him. What does God promise to give those who humble themselves in repentance and turn back to Him (see verse 6)?

_____

_____

_____

_____

_____

_____

_____

_____

_____

_____

_____

Submit to God (James 4:7–12)

⁷ Therefore submit to God. Resist the devil and he will flee from you. ⁸ Draw near to God and He will draw near to you. Cleanse your hands, you sinners; and purify your hearts, you double-minded. ⁹ Lament and mourn and weep! Let your laughter be turned to mourning and your joy to gloom. ¹⁰ Humble yourselves in the sight of the Lord, and He will lift you up.

¹¹ Do not speak evil of one another, brethren. He who speaks evil of a brother and judges his brother, speaks evil of the law and judges the law. But if you judge the law, you are not a doer of the law but a judge. ¹² There is one Lawgiver, who is able to save and to destroy. Who are you to judge another?

7. What commands does James issue as it relates to submitting to God and resisting the devil? What promise is given for those who humble themselves before the Lord (see verses 7–10)?

_____

_____

_____

_____

_____

_____

_____

8. What does James say about judging our fellow brothers and sisters in Christ? What are we actually doing when we judge others (see verses 11–12)?

_____

_____

_____

_____

_____

_____

_____

_____

REVIEWING THE STORY

Paul closes his first letter to the Thessalonians with a series of exhortations, blessings, and admonitions. He emphasizes the importance of believers continuing to work—and to recognize those who labor among them and are in authority over them—as they await Jesus' return. He urges the workers in the Thessalonian church to reestablish peace and fellowship with those who had ditched their responsibilities in order to wait for Christ's return. He offers a series of instructions to help the Thessalonians continue to grow in their Christian faith, pronounces a final blessing from God over them, and charges them to read his letter aloud in the church.

9. How should we respond when someone does evil toward us (see 1 Thessalonians 5:15)?

_____

_____

_____

_____

_____

10. How can we resist the influence of false teachers (see 1 Thessalonians 5:21–22)?

_____

_____

_____

_____

_____

11. What personal request does Paul make of the Thessalonian believers (see 1 Thessalonians 5:25)?

_____

_____

_____

_____

_____

12. What does Paul want the Thessalonians to do with his letter (see 1 Thessalonians 5:27)?

_____

_____

_____

_____

_____

_____

_____

_____

_____

_____

APPLYING THE MESSAGE

13. Who is someone in your church who has been faithful in ministry? How can you recognize that person's efforts and encourage him or her?

_____

_____

_____

_____

_____

_____

_____

_____

_____

_____

14. What are some areas in your life where you need to be more "patient with all" (1 Thessalonians 5:14)? How can you work toward being more patient with others?

_____

_____

_____

_____

_____

_____

_____

_____

_____

Reflecting on the Meaning

Paul closes his first letter to Thessalonians with a list of three things we are to do that fall within God's will for our lives. First, *we are to be filled with joy* (see 1 Thessalonians 5:16). This instruction is not optional but a *command*—and is something we are to do continually. Even in times of great difficulty and crisis, we can experience great joy, because the joy that we have is founded not on our situation but on our relationship with Christ.

Second, *we are to be fervent in prayer* (see verse 17). Paul states that we are to pray "without ceasing," which means that we remain in a continual state of communication with God. Prayer is our lifeline to heaven, and there should never be a time when we are out of contact with our heavenly Father. We must remain continually in a spirit of prayer.

Third, *we are to be faithful in thanksgiving* (see verse 18). God desires for us to rejoice, pray, and be thankful. It is not His will for us to walk unhappy, unbowed, and ungrateful. It's wonderful to be around people who rejoice, pray, and express gratitude. It's refreshing to be in their midst. We should strive to be those kind of people to others in our world.

JOURNALING YOUR RESPONSE

What tends to get in the way of you having a joyful attitude, praying regularly, and expressing gratitude to God for His blessings? What can you do today to remove those obstacles?

STANDING STRONG IN TRIBULATION

2 Thessalonians 1:1–12

GETTING STARTED

How have challenges in your life helped you to better understand the grace and mercy of God?

_____

_____

_____

_____

_____

_____

_____

_____

_____

_____

_____

_____

_____

_____

_____

_____

_____

_____

SETTING THE STAGE

Sometime after Paul sent his first letter to the church in Thessalonica, the believers there received another letter whose author *claimed* to be Paul. This letter contained some disturbing claims—namely, that the believers had missed the Rapture and were now living in the Tribulation period! The letter explained that this was the reason why the Thessalonian believers were experiencing trials, persecution, and suffering.

The misinformation presented in this forged letter prompted Paul to write a second *genuine* letter to the believers in the city. He addresses the issue head-on with these words: "Now, brethren, concerning the coming of our Lord Jesus Christ and our gathering together to Him, we ask you, not to be soon shaken in mind or troubled, either by spirit or by word or by letter, as if from us, as though the day of Christ had come" (2 Thessalonians 2:1–2).

In other words, the believers were not to allow *anyone* to deceive them into believing they were in the midst of the Tribulation. In fact, if you read to the end of 2 Thessalonians, you will find that Paul is careful to make sure they know this letter is actually from him. He tells them, in effect, "Notice that it's my own handwriting in this letter."

Paul thus writes this second letter to correct errors that had cropped up in the church and to encourage the believers to endure persecution. He shows them that certain things must take place before the Tribulation can occur. In the process, he reveals that as impressive as the Thessalonians were in their faith, they were not above making mistakes in their doctrine.

EXPLORING THE TEXT

Paul's Opening Words (2 Thessalonians 1:1–8)

¹ Paul, Silvanus, and Timothy,

To the church of the Thessalonians in God our Father and the Lord Jesus Christ:

² Grace to you and peace from God our Father and the Lord Jesus Christ.

³ We are bound to thank God always for you, brethren, as it is fitting, because your faith grows exceedingly, and the love of every one of you all abounds toward each other, ⁴ so that we ourselves boast of you among the churches of God for your patience and faith in all your persecutions and tribulations that you endure, ⁵ which is manifest evidence of the righteous judgment of God, that you may be counted worthy of the kingdom of God, for which you also suffer; ⁶ since it is a righteous thing with God to repay with tribulation those who trouble you, ⁷ and to give you who are troubled rest with us when the Lord Jesus is revealed from heaven with His mighty angels, ⁸ in flaming fire taking vengeance on those who do not know God, and on those who do not obey the gospel of our Lord Jesus Christ.

---

1. In Paul's first letter to the Thessalonians, he noted the "afflictions" they were facing (see 1 Thessalonians 3:1–5). Here, in this second letter to the same church, he addresses the "persecutions and tribulations" they were continuing to endure (see 2 Thessalonians 1:4). How does Paul say that he and his fellow missionaries have used the experiences of the Thessalonian believers to inspire other churches (verses 3–5)?

_____

_____

_____

_____

_____

_____

_____

_____

_____

2. Paul assures the Thessalonian believers that the persecution they were suffering was evidence of their perseverance in the faith, not punishment because of their sin. How does Paul compare the believers with their persecutors (see verses 5–8)?

_____

_____

_____

_____

God's Final Judgment and Glory (2 Thessalonians 1:9–12)

⁹ These shall be punished with everlasting destruction from the presence of the Lord and from the glory of His power, ¹⁰ when He comes, in that Day, to be glorified in His saints and to be admired among all those who believe, because our testimony among you was believed.

¹¹ Therefore we also pray always for you that our God would count you worthy of this calling, and fulfill all the good pleasure of His goodness and the work of faith with power, ¹² that the name of our Lord Jesus Christ may be glorified in you, and you in Him, according to the grace of our God and the Lord Jesus Christ.

3. Paul defines "everlasting destruction" as separation from God's presence and His glory. What reassurance does Paul give to the Thessalonian believers to convince them of the salvation they will experience on the day of the Lord (see 2 Thessalonians 1:9–10)?

_____

_____

_____

_____

4. Paul concludes the section with a brief prayer for the believers. What is Paul's request to God for them? What does he want God to fulfill in them (see verses 11–12)?

_____

_____

_____

_____

_____

_____

_____

_____

_____

_____

GOING DEEPER

A rumor had circulated in the Thessalonian church that the trials the believers were facing meant they were going through the Tribulation. Paul corrects this misunderstanding by dismissing any such connection between their trials and the Tribulation, providing key details about what must first take place before the Tribulation can occur. Jesus likewise spoke about the events that would precede the Tribulation. In doing so, He draws on prophecy from Daniel to sketch a scene of unremitting and inescapable horror. He adds that no one on earth knows when this day and hour will come—so His followers must keep watch and stay vigilant.

The Great Tribulation (Matthew 24:15–28)

15 "Therefore when you see the 'abomination of desolation,' spoken of by Daniel the prophet, standing in the holy place" (whoever reads, let him understand), 16 "then let those who are in Judea flee to the mountains. 17 Let him who is on the housetop not go down to take anything out of his house. 18 And let him who is in the field not go

back to get his clothes. ¹⁹ But woe to those who are pregnant and to those who are nursing babies in those days! ²⁰ And pray that your flight may not be in winter or on the Sabbath. ²¹ For then there will be great tribulation, such as has not been since the beginning of the world until this time, no, nor ever shall be. ²² And unless those days were shortened, no flesh would be saved; but for the elect's sake those days will be shortened.

²³ "Then if anyone says to you, 'Look, here is the Christ!' or 'There!' do not believe it. ²⁴ For false christs and false prophets will rise and show great signs and wonders to deceive, if possible, even the elect. ²⁵ See, I have told you beforehand.

²⁶ "Therefore if they say to you, 'Look, He is in the desert!' do not go out; or 'Look, He is in the inner rooms!' do not believe it. ²⁷ For as the lightning comes from the east and flashes to the west, so also will the coming of the Son of Man be. ²⁸ For wherever the carcass is, there the eagles will be gathered together."

---

5. Daniel prophesies about the "abomination of desolation" (verse 15; see also Daniel 8:13; 9:27; 11:31), to which Jesus refers. How does Jesus describe this time of destruction? What hope does He offer to those who would experience it (see Matthew 24:15–22)?

_____

_____

_____

_____

_____

_____

_____

_____

_____

_____

6. Jesus warns that people will be deceived by false prophets and others falsely claiming to be the Christ during the Tribulation (see verses 23–26). Yet He makes it clear that His actual return will be unmistakable. How does Jesus describe His second coming (see verses 27–28)?

_____

_____

_____

_____

_____

_____

The Day and Hour Unknown (Matthew 24:36–44)

36 "But of that day and hour no one knows, not even the angels of heaven, but My Father only. 37 But as the days of Noah were, so also will the coming of the Son of Man be. 38 For as in the days before the flood, they were eating and drinking, marrying and giving in marriage, until the day that Noah entered the ark, 39 and did not know until the flood came and took them all away, so also will the coming of the Son of Man be. 40 Then two men will be in the field: one will be taken and the other left. 41 Two women will be grinding at the mill: one will be taken and the other left. 42 Watch therefore, for you do not know what hour your Lord is coming. 43 But know this, that if the master of the house had known what hour the thief would come, he would have watched and not allowed his house to be broken into. 44 Therefore you also be ready, for the Son of Man is coming at an hour you do not expect.

7. Jesus states that only God the Father knows when the events of the Great Tribulation will take place in this world. However, there are signs that indicate this time is arriving. How does Jesus use the example of the Great Flood to illustrate the attitude that people will have in the days preceding the Tribulation? What behaviors will they exhibit (see verses 36–39)?

_____

_____

_____

_____

_____

8. What will happen to those who are not faithfully watching and waiting for Jesus' return? What is the warning and command for believers today (see verses 42–44)?

_____

_____

_____

_____

_____

REVIEWING THE STORY

Paul begins his second letter to the believers in Thessalonica in much the same way as he began his first letter. He states that the believers there are the reason for his continual thankfulness to God. He has been spreading the news wherever he goes about their love for one another and their faithfulness in the midst of tribulation. He then helps the Thessalonians understand that their present trials and suffering are evidence of God's extraordinary work in their lives. He looks ahead to the second coming of Christ and God's final judgment in order to comfort the Thessalonian believers, encourage them, and motivate them to continue in their faithfulness.

9. For what reason were the Thessalonian believers suffering
(see 2 Thessalonians 1:5)?

_____

_____

_____

_____

_____

_____

10. What will happen to those who avoid suffering for God's kingdom
by rejecting His gospel (see 2 Thessalonians 1:7–9)?

_____

_____

_____

_____

_____

_____

11. Why does Paul say the Thessalonian believers will be counted
among the saints (see 2 Thessalonians 1:10)?

_____

_____

_____

_____

_____

12. What was Paul's prayer for the Thessalonians (see 2 Thessalonians 1:11–12)?

_____

_____

_____

_____

_____

APPLYING THE MESSAGE

13. What trials or tribulations are currently testing your strength and endurance?

_____

_____

_____

_____

_____

_____

14. How do Paul's words to the Thessalonians encourage you to stand strong in the midst of your trials?

_____

_____

_____

_____

_____

_____

REFLECTING ON THE MEANING

Paul's opening words in this second letter to the Thessalonians are typical of what we find in his other epistles. He offers "grace . . . and peace from God" to an unsettled group of Christians who were facing persecution for their faith (2 Thessalonians 1:2). Paul then goes on to explain three ways he is encouraged as he considers how they have persevered through these trials.

First, Paul is encouraged because of their faith. Paul writes, "We are bound to thank God always for you, brethren, as it is fitting, because your faith grows exceedingly" (verse 3). In spite of the suffering the Thessalonians were enduring, their faith was growing and spreading. Paul could actually boast about them to his other churches (see verse 4). One commentator notes that praise from a person you respect never leaves you feeling *proud* but *humbled*. It makes you want to do better so that you can live up to the praise heaped on you by that person. This was certainly the case for the believers in Thessalonica when they received this praise from Paul.

Second, Paul is encouraged because of their love. Paul notes, "The love of every one of you all abounds toward each other"(verse 3). Not only were the Thessalonians faithful, but they were loving as well. This was an answer to the prayer Paul prayed in his first letter, where he asked God to help them abound in love toward one another (see 1 Thessalonians 3:12). The believers had learned to love one another in the midst of difficult times. They had continued to extend themselves for the good of each other in spite of the adversity they faced.

Third, Paul is encouraged because of their patience. He states, "We ourselves boast of you among the churches of God for your patience and faith in all your persecutions and tribulations" (verse 4). Paul praises the believers for the way they have behaved under strain—not only because of the persecutions they were enduring for their faith, but also because of the way they were standing strong under the everyday tribulations of life. In all things, both great and small, they were living with great patience.

JOURNALING YOUR RESPONSE

How has a trial in your life served as an opportunity to make your faith apparent to others?

THE ANTICHRIST IS COMING

2 Thessalonians 2:1–8

GETTING STARTED

What images come to mind when you hear the term "Antichrist"?

_____

_____

_____

_____

_____

_____

_____

_____

_____

_____

_____

SETTING THE STAGE

Throughout history, whenever a particularly polarizing person has stepped onto the world stage, people have often accused him of being the "Antichrist." For instance, when John F. Kennedy embarked on his presidential campaign in 1960, some people decided he was a good candidate for the Antichrist because he had been wounded in the war (drawing on imagery from Revelation 13:3). In the late twentieth century, many thought Henry Kissinger might be the Antichrist. Others have pointed to various popes. Truth be told, just about anyone can be a prime candidate to be the Antichrist if you find the right method for determining it.

To illustrate, we could use a method called *gematria* to "prove" that Adolf Hitler was the Antichrist. Under this method, certain numbers are associated with letters in the alphabet. It's a bit complicated, but if you begin with 100 and assign each letter with a corresponding numerical value (A = 100; B = 101; C = 102), you come up with the following for "Hitler": H = 107; I = 108; T = 119; L = 111; E = 104; and R = 117. Add all of these numbers together, and you come up with a sum of 666—the number of the Antichrist! So, Hitler must *be* the Antichrist.

In truth, by using various numerical schemes, you can make practically anyone the Antichrist. But the bottom line is this: we don't know exactly who he is. We only know this—the Antichrist will rise upon the stage of world history and play the dominant role in end-time history as the leader of those who stand in opposition to the work and will of God.

In this lesson, you will examine Paul's teaching regarding the rise of the Antichrist and the coming Tribulation on earth. And you will discover yet another reason for Christians to rejoice in God's plan to remove them from the earth before the Antichrist rises to power.

EXPLORING THE TEXT

The Falling Away (2 Thessalonians 2:1–4)

¹ Now, brethren, concerning the coming of our Lord Jesus Christ and our gathering together to Him, we ask you, ² not to be soon shaken in mind or troubled, either by spirit or by word or by letter, as if from us, as though the day of Christ had come. ³ Let no one deceive you by any means; for that Day will not come unless the falling away

comes first, and the man of sin is revealed, the son of perdition, [4] who opposes and exalts himself above all that is called God or that is worshiped, so that he sits as God in the temple of God, showing himself that he is God.

---

1. As previously noted, at some point after the Thessalonians received Paul's first letter, they were persuaded by someone falsely claiming to be Paul that Jesus' second coming had already occurred. What effect did this deception have on the Thessalonian believers (see verses 1–3)?

_____

_____

_____

_____

2. Paul assertively denies any involvement in deceiving the Thessalonian believers concerning the day of the Lord, which he insists has not yet occurred. According to Paul, what events will precede Jesus' second coming (see verses 3–4)?

_____

_____

_____

_____

_____

The Mystery of Lawlessness (2 Thessalonians 2:5–8)

[5] Do you not remember that when I was still with you I told you these things? [6] And now you know what is restraining, that he may be revealed in his own time. [7] For the mystery of lawlessness is already at work; only He who now restrains will do so until He is taken out

of the way. [8] And then the lawless one will be revealed, whom the Lord will consume with the breath of His mouth and destroy with the brightness of His coming.

3. Paul had previously taught the Thessalonians about the day of the Lord (see verse 5), so he leaves out details that would have helped us identify the "restrainer" and what is being restrained. Many believe Paul is alluding to the Holy Spirit, who indwelled believers at Pentecost, but who will depart from them at the Tribulation. What does Paul say will happen when the restraining power is removed (see verses 6–8)?

_____

_____

_____

_____

4. With the absence of the Holy Spirit's presence in this world, the lawless one (or Antichrist) will unleash destruction on the earth. However, at the close of the Tribulation period, how will the Lord Jesus ultimately put an end to the destruction (see verse 8)?

_____

_____

_____

_____

GOING DEEPER

In addition to the apostle Paul, the disciple John makes reference to an individual or spirit that he calls the "Antichrist" in his letters. In his first letter, John sounds the alarm about false teachers in the church who try to lead believers astray (much like the false teachers in Thessalonica were leading those believers astray). John encourages all believers in Christ to "test the spirits" (the teaching they are receiving) so as not to be deceived.

The Spirit of Truth and Spirit of Error (1 John 4:1–6)

[1] Beloved, do not believe every spirit, but test the spirits, whether they are of God; because many false prophets have gone out into the world. [2] By this you know the Spirit of God: Every spirit that confesses that Jesus Christ has come in the flesh is of God, [3] and every spirit that does not confess that Jesus Christ has come in the flesh is not of God. And this is the spirit of the Antichrist, which you have heard was coming, and is now already in the world.

[4] You are of God, little children, and have overcome them, because He who is in you is greater than he who is in the world. [5] They are of the world. Therefore they speak as of the world, and the world hears them. [6] We are of God. He who knows God hears us; he who is not of God does not hear us. By this we know the spirit of truth and the spirit of error.

5. John presents all teaching as having a spiritual dimension—it is either true ("of God"), or it is false ("not of God"). What does he urge believers in Christ to do to identify the spirit of the Antichrist and ensure that what they are hearing is from God (see verses 1–3)?

6. John uses "the world" to refer to all people who reject Jesus as God's Son and who oppose Christians. How are followers of Jesus different from those in "the world"? What promise does John provide as it relates to God hearing our prayers (see verses 4–6)?

Beware of Antichrist Deceivers (2 John 1:7–11)

7 For many deceivers have gone out into the world who do not confess Jesus Christ as coming in the flesh. This is a deceiver and an antichrist. 8 Look to yourselves, that we do not lose those things we worked for, but that we may receive a full reward.

9 Whoever transgresses and does not abide in the doctrine of Christ does not have God. He who abides in the doctrine of Christ has both the Father and the Son. 10 If anyone comes to you and does not bring this doctrine, do not receive him into your house nor greet him; 11 for he who greets him shares in his evil deeds.

---

7. John's statement about the Antichrist mirrors his words in Revelation 20:8: "[Satan] will go out to deceive the nations." What does John say these deceivers will do? What actions should believers in Christ take to guard against being deceived (see verses 7–8)?

----

8. How does John say that we will be able to recognize a person who is a "deceiver and an antichrist"? How should Christians regard such individuals (see verses 9–11)?

_____

_____

_____

_____

REVIEWING THE STORY

Paul points out to the believers in Thessalonica that they had been tricked into believing they were now living in the Tribulation. He sets them straight by revealing certain things that must happen before the Tribulation occurs. One of the key figures of this time is the Antichrist, or "lawless one," who is currently being restrained (likely by the Holy Spirit). The Tribulation will not occur until that restraining force is removed. Paul then comforts the Thessalonians by giving them signs to look for that will help them anticipate and prepare for Christ's coming.

9. What is Paul's purpose in writing to the Thessalonian believers about the coming of the Lord Jesus Christ (see 2 Thessalonians 2:1–2)?

_____

_____

_____

_____

10. What assurance does Paul provide to calm the believers' fears that Jesus had already returned and they were going through the Tribulation (see 2 Thessalonians 2:3)?

_____

_____

_____

11. Why is Paul surprised, and perhaps a little disappointed, that the Thessalonian believers had allowed themselves to be deceived by an impostor (see 2 Thessalonians 2:5)?

_____

_____

_____

_____

_____

_____

12. When will the lawless one—the Antichrist—be revealed (see 2 Thessalonians 2:7–8)?

_____

_____

_____

_____

_____

_____

APPLYING THE MESSAGE

13. What are some ways that you can guard against being deceived by false teachings?

_____

_____

_____

_____

_____

_____

_____

14. Why is it important for you personally to understand events concerning the end times?

_____

_____

_____

_____

_____

REFLECTING ON THE MEANING

In this section of Paul's second letter to the Thessalonians, he encourages believers to remain faithful in their anticipation of Jesus' coming by holding fast to the truth of the gospel. The good news for believers in this discussion of the end times is that God is in control. The Tribulation will occur because it is part of His plan. Those who experience it will be those who refuse to believe the truth—those who take pleasure in unrighteousness instead of enjoying God.

So, while we might talk about the role of the Antichrist in God's plan, there is no need for us to search out obscure clues about his identity. As believers in Christ , we will not encounter him. We will be gone when he steps onto the world stage. As Paul states, we are better off "looking for the blessed hope and glorious appearing of our great God and Savior Jesus Christ" (Titus 2:13). Our future is wrapped up not in the Antichrist but in the Lord Jesus Christ. One day He will come for us, so we need to be always looking for Him.

Christian author Donald Grey Barnhouse tells the story of how one morning during the Christmas season he awoke and went to the piano in his home. He started to play "Silent Night" but then purposely stopped before playing the last note. He then walked into the hallway and listened to the sounds that came from the upstairs in his house. His eight-year-old son had stopped reading and was trying to find the final note on his harmonica. Another child was singing the note. Someone else came downstairs and asked, "Did you do that on purpose?"

For Christians, our whole song has been played—except for the last note. We know there has been no resolution to our song. So we wait, and long for, that last note to be struck.

JOURNALING YOUR RESPONSE

How would you describe your longing for Jesus' return?

_____

_____

_____

_____

_____

_____

_____

_____

_____

_____

_____

_____

_____

_____

_____

_____

_____

_____

_____

_____

_____

_____

TRUTH FOR TROUBLED TIMES

2 Thessalonians 2:9–17

GETTING STARTED

What is the most comforting thing that someone has said to you during a difficult or troubling time in your life?

_____

_____

_____

_____

_____

_____

_____

_____

_____

_____

_____

_____

_____

_____

_____

_____

_____

SETTING THE STAGE

No one gets out of this world without experiencing trouble. Mercifully, most of the trouble that we will face is manageable and short-lived. Occasionally, however, we will run into protracted periods of trouble—the kind with no good end in sight. Extended illnesses fall into this category, as do addictions, serious family problems, and marital discord. Some problems never seem to be resolved, which make them seem absolutely devastating.

We can face the challenges that come for a moment. We can find hope—from a friend, or from a family member, or even from our own internal wellspring of optimism. But what do we do when we have been experiencing trouble for a long time? And how do we help other people in our lives get through their prolonged periods of distress? Easy answers won't get the job done. Trite responses aren't going to help. More is needed than just simple and easy-to-grasp answers. We need *answers* from the Word of God.

We find those answers in this next section of Paul's letter. As we saw in the previous lesson, Paul corrected the Thessalonian believers' misunderstandings about the end times and presented some rather dark prophecies for those who refuse to trust in Christ. Now, as is often the case in Paul's letters, he turns from discussing matters of doctrine to matters of practical living. He encourages the believers—and us—to stand fast in the truth of God's Word and turn to it for answers. As we do, we will experience true comfort from the Lord in our time of need.

EXPLORING THE TEXT

The Great Apostasy (2 Thessalonians 2:9–12)

⁹ The coming of the lawless one is according to the working of Satan, with all power, signs, and lying wonders, ¹⁰ and with all unrighteous deception among those who perish, because they did not receive the love of the truth, that they might be saved. ¹¹ And for this reason

God will send them strong delusion, that they should believe the lie, [12] that they all may be condemned who did not believe the truth but had pleasure in unrighteousness.

---

1. Paul describes the Antichrist, "the lawless one," as a counterfeit Christ who will deceive people into thinking he is doing good through various signs and wonders that he performs. As Paul said to the Corinthians, "Satan himself transforms himself into an angel of light" (2 Corinthians 11:14), and the Antichrist will deceive people in much the same way. Why are the unrighteous susceptible to the Antichrist's deception (see 2 Thessalonians 2:9–11)?

_____

_____

_____

_____

_____

_____

_____

_____

_____

_____

_____

_____

_____

_____

_____

_____

2. Paul wrote to the Romans, "Even as [the unrighteous] did not like to retain God in their knowledge, God gave them over to . . . do those things which are not fitting" (Romans 1:28). Similarly, here Paul emphasizes that God's judgment on those who are deceived by the lawless one is in *response* to the people's deliberate refusal to believe the truth. What is the mindset that blinds people to the consequences of their actions (see 2 Thessalonians 2:12)?

_____

_____

_____

_____

_____

_____

_____

_____

_____

_____

Stand Fast (2 Thessalonians 2:13–17)

13 But we are bound to give thanks to God always for you, brethren beloved by the Lord, because God from the beginning chose you for salvation through sanctification by the Spirit and belief in the truth, 14 to which He called you by our gospel, for the obtaining of the glory of our Lord Jesus Christ. 15 Therefore, brethren, stand fast and hold the traditions which you were taught, whether by word or our epistle.

16 Now may our Lord Jesus Christ Himself, and our God and Father, who has loved us and given us everlasting consolation and good hope by grace, 17 comfort your hearts and establish you in every good word and work.

3. Paul now turns from discussing the consequences for those who choose not to believe the truth of the gospel to reassuring the Thessalonian believers that their salvation is secure. What role does Paul say that the Holy Spirit plays in our salvation (see verses 13–14)?

_____

_____

_____

_____

_____

_____

_____

4. Paul tells the believers to "stand fast" in their faith and "hold the traditions which [they] were taught" (verse 15). In this context, traditions refer to the truth of the gospel. How were the Thessalonians taught these traditions? How would they receive comfort and encouragement as they continued forward in their faith (see verses 15–17)?

_____

_____

_____

_____

_____

_____

_____

_____

_____

GOING DEEPER

The apostle Paul was no stranger to trials and difficulties. He frequently faced opposition for sharing the gospel, was misunderstood by friends and opponents alike, and endured imprisonments and beatings. However, Paul was able to persevere because he knew there was a greater glory waiting for him after his time on earth was finished. For Paul, the trials of this world were but a drop in the bucket compared to what lay ahead for him in eternity. In his letter to the Romans, he expounds on this future glory that awaits all believers in Christ and the incredible sacrifice that God had to make so we could obtain salvation and eternal life.

Christ in Our Place (Romans 5:5–11)

⁵ Now hope does not disappoint, because the love of God has been poured out in our hearts by the Holy Spirit who was given to us.

⁶ For when we were still without strength, in due time Christ died for the ungodly. ⁷ For scarcely for a righteous man will one die; yet perhaps for a good man someone would even dare to die. ⁸ But God demonstrates His own love toward us, in that while we were still sinners, Christ died for us. ⁹ Much more then, having now been justified by His blood, we shall be saved from wrath through Him. ¹⁰ For if when we were enemies we were reconciled to God through the death of His Son, much more, having been reconciled, we shall be saved by His life. ¹¹ And not only that, but we also rejoice in God through our Lord Jesus Christ, through whom we have now received the reconciliation.

5. Our hope as believers is unshakable because of what God has done for us through Jesus, and we have assurance of His love for us because of the presence of the Holy Spirit within us. For whom does Paul say that

Christ died? Why is it significant that God chose to sacrifice His only Son even when we were "sinners" and His "enemies" (see verses 5–8)?

_____

_____

_____

_____

_____

_____

_____

_____

6. Our confidence in God's love for us is strengthened not only because of what God will do for us by sparing us from His future wrath but also because of the relationship we have with Him in the present. Given this, why can we rejoice even in trials (see verses 9–11)?

_____

_____

_____

_____

_____

_____

_____

_____

From Suffering to Glory (Romans 8:18–25)

18 For I consider that the sufferings of this present time are not worthy to be compared with the glory which shall be revealed in us. 19 For the

earnest expectation of the creation eagerly waits for the revealing of the sons of God. [20] For the creation was subjected to futility, not willingly, but because of Him who subjected it in hope; [21] because the creation itself also will be delivered from the bondage of corruption into the glorious liberty of the children of God. [22] For we know that the whole creation groans and labors with birth pangs together until now. [23] Not only that, but we also who have the firstfruits of the Spirit, even we ourselves groan within ourselves, eagerly waiting for the adoption, the redemption of our body. [24] For we were saved in this hope, but hope that is seen is not hope; for why does one still hope for what he sees? [25] But if we hope for what we do not see, we eagerly wait for it with perseverance.

---

7. Not long before Jesus' arrest and crucifixion, He told His disciples, "These things I have spoken to you, that in Me you may have peace. In the world you will have tribulation; but be of good cheer, I have overcome the world" (John 16:33). What is Paul's perspective on the trouble and sufferings we experience in this world (see Romans 8:18–21)?

_____

_____

_____

_____

_____

_____

_____

_____

_____

_____

_____

8. Paul notes that creation also suffers as a result of sin and decay in the world. As humans, and as believers, we are part of creation and will not escape chaos, pain, and suffering. What hope does Paul give regarding the future restoration of both believers and creation? What attitude should believers have as they wait for this restoration (see verses 22–25)?

_____

_____

_____

_____

_____

REVIEWING THE STORY

Paul writes that the Antichrist, empowered by Satan, will come with "signs, and lying wonders" (2 Thessalonians 2:9) to deceive people and cause them to reject God's salvation. Many will believe his lies and be condemned to God's judgment. Paul expresses his gratitude to God that the Thessalonians will not be among them, for God has chosen them for salvation—and they have accepted His call. He urges the believers to continue to stand fast in the midst of their troubles and to hold firm to the truths of God that they had been taught.

9. Why will people perish during the final judgment (see 2 Thessalonians 2:10)?

_____

_____

_____

_____

_____

_____

10. What will God do to those who do "not receive the love of truth, that they might be saved" (see 2 Thessalonians 2:10–12)?

_____

_____

_____

_____

11. Why can we trust Jesus Christ and God the Father to see us through troubled times (see 2 Thessalonians 2:16)?

_____

_____

_____

_____

12. What does Paul pray the Lord will do for the Thessalonian believers, who were facing serious trouble (see 2 Thessalonians 2:17)?

_____

_____

_____

_____

APPLYING THE MESSAGE

13. How do you respond to the idea that "God from the beginning chose you for salvation" (2 Thessalonians 2:13)? Do you find this difficult or easy to accept? Explain.

_____

_____

_____

_____

14. How does Paul's teaching in 2 Thessalonians 2:9–17, Romans 5:5–11, and Romans 8:18–25 encourage you to deal with trouble in life?

REFLECTING ON THE MEANING

In this section of Paul's letter, he warns the believers in Thessalonica to be wary of the deception of Satan and the lawless one. He encourages them to live in light of the future hope they have received because of the truth they have been taught. As we look at Paul's words, we find there are at least two actions we can take in response to this hope we have been given.

First, we can give thanks to God for the gift of salvation. Paul writes, "God from the beginning chose you for salvation through sanctification by the Spirit and belief in the truth" (2 Thessalonians 2:13). God has given us not only salvation but also the Holy Spirit, who remains with us as we live and work in this world. As we consider the depths of these incredible gifts, we express our gratitude to God in spite of the circumstances we are facing.

Second, we can stand fast in the truth of God's Word. Paul states, "Stand fast and hold the traditions which you were taught, whether by word or our epistle" (verse 15). His use of the term *traditions* refers to spiritual truths passed from generation to generation. The believers in Paul's day received truth through oral tradition or through his letters. Paul wants them to stand firm and not lose sight of what they had been taught. In the same way, we are to hold God's truth firmly and never let it slip from us, regardless of the trials that come into our lives.

We may not understand everything that is happening in our lives in the moment. We may never know the reason why we had to endure certain trials and times of suffering. However, through the Word of God, we can be sure God is always in control and has a plan for us. As we come to this knowledge, we find a new perspective on our trouble. We discover that we

117

can stand fast—and actually thrive—in the midst of those trials. And as we stand fast in the traditions of the Word of God, we are kept from being deceived by anyone or anything that seeks to lure us away from the gospel.

JOURNALING YOUR RESPONSE

What truths of God's Word have you built your life around?

_____

_____

_____

_____

_____

_____

_____

_____

_____

_____

_____

_____

_____

_____

_____

_____

_____

_____

_____

_____

_____

_____

_____

GOD IS ALWAYS FAITHFUL

2 Thessalonians 3:1–9

GETTING STARTED

What are some ways that people have proven to be faithful to you?

_____

_____

_____

_____

_____

_____

_____

_____

_____

_____

_____

_____

_____

_____

_____

_____

_____

_____

_____

_____

_____

SETTING THE STAGE

Unfaithfulness seems to be prevalent in our day. In the business world, a person's word no longer means much. In the media, once-reliable sources for news and entertainment can no longer be trusted. In marriages, "till death do us part" are often just words in a ceremony. Even among Christians, commitments are made and broken with little conscience.

Centuries ago, the wise King Solomon asked, "Who can find a faithful man?" (Proverbs 20:6). Good question! Where can we find a faithful person? Where can we find someone who will do what he or she says? The search in our world would be long and exhausting. Whether we care to admit it or not, each of us is guilty of unfaithfulness in one form or another. Each of us, at some point in our lives, has given someone else reason not to trust us to do what we say.

The apostle Paul addresses the issue of faithfulness in his final chapter of 2 Thessalonians. He presents to us the One who never forgets, never fails, never falters, always keeps His word, is faithful at all times and in everything—and who will never, ever change. Although people become unfaithful due to desire, fear, weakness, loss of interest, or outside influence, our heavenly Father is impervious to all these things. He cannot be turned from His faithfulness.

Paul uses just four words to express this truth: "the Lord is faithful" (2 Thessalonians 3:3). It is simply stated, yet all the books ever written could not contain the universe of implications, possibilities, and applications that spring from this single important truth.

EXPLORING THE TEXT

Pray for Us (2 Thessalonians 3:1–5)

---

¹ Finally, brethren, pray for us, that the word of the Lord may run swiftly and be glorified, just as it is with you, ² and that we may be delivered from unreasonable and wicked men; for not all have faith.

³ But the Lord is faithful, who will establish you and guard you from the evil one. ⁴ And we have confidence in the Lord concerning you, both that you do and will do the things we command you.

⁵ Now may the Lord direct your hearts into the love of God and into the patience of Christ.

---

1. Paul contrasts the widespread lack of faith among people with the faithfulness of Jesus. What can believers count on the Lord to do because He is faithful (see verses 1–3)?

_____

_____

_____

_____

_____

_____

_____

2. Paul compliments the Thessalonians' faithfulness to the Lord, but he doesn't want them to think they are self-sufficient in standing fast in their faith. What does Paul ask the Lord to do for them in his prayer for the believers (see verses 4–5)?

_____

_____

_____

_____

_____

_____

_____

Setting an Example Through Hard Work
(2 Thessalonians 3:6–9)

⁶ But we command you, brethren, in the name of our Lord Jesus Christ, that you withdraw from every brother who walks disorderly and not according to the tradition which he received from us. ⁷ For you yourselves know how you ought to follow us, for we were not disorderly among you; ⁸ nor did we eat anyone's bread free of charge, but worked with labor and toil night and day, that we might not be a burden to any of you, ⁹ not because we do not have authority, but to make ourselves an example of how you should follow us.

3. Paul's statement, "every brother who walks disorderly," refers to those in the Thessalonian church who were embracing idleness and refusing to work. What are Paul's instructions to the church members about how to deal with these individuals (see verse 6)?

4. Paul worked hard as a tentmaker (see Acts 18:3) and in fulfilling his duties as an apostle. Why did he insist on earning his keep, doing double duty with his responsibilities between work and ministry, during his stay in Thessalonica (see 2 Thessalonians 3:7–9)?

_____

_____

_____

_____

_____

_____

_____

_____

_____

_____

GOING DEEPER

The Lord has always been faithful to His people. We find this truth throughout Scripture, where the Lord frequently reminds His followers that He will stay true to His promises. Sadly, in the history of God's people, it was always the *people* who were unfaithful to God. In the book of Deuteronomy, we find the following truths from Moses about the way God considers His people and His promise to remain faithful to them. We also find several truths about the blessings that we can expect if we choose to likewise remain faithful and obedient to God.

A Chosen People (Deuteronomy 7:6–12)

⁶ "For you are a holy people to the LORD your God; the LORD your God has chosen you to be a people for Himself, a special treasure above all the peoples on the face of the earth. ⁷ The LORD did not set His love on you nor choose you because you were more in number

than any other people, for you were the least of all peoples; ⁸ but because the Lᴏʀᴅ loves you, and because He would keep the oath which He swore to your fathers, the Lᴏʀᴅ has brought you out with a mighty hand, and redeemed you from the house of bondage, from the hand of Pharaoh king of Egypt.

⁹ "Therefore know that the Lᴏʀᴅ your God, He is God, the faithful God who keeps covenant and mercy for a thousand generations with those who love Him and keep His commandments; ¹⁰ and He repays those who hate Him to their face, to destroy them. He will not be slack with him who hates Him; He will repay him to his face. ¹¹ Therefore you shall keep the commandment, the statutes, and the judgments which I command you today, to observe them.

¹² "Then it shall come to pass, because you listen to these judgments, and keep and do them, that the Lᴏʀᴅ your God will keep with you the covenant and the mercy which He swore to your fathers."

---

5. Moses issued these declarations to the Israelites as they were preparing to enter into the Promised Land. How does Moses say that God viewed the people of Israel? On what basis did He choose them and extend His love to them (see verses 6–8)?

_____

_____

_____

_____

_____

_____

_____

_____

_____

_____

_____

_____

6. What does Moses say about God's faithfulness? Why was it important for the Israelites to obey God's commands if they wanted to experience His blessings (see verses 9–12)?

_____

_____

_____

_____

_____

_____

_____

_____

_____

_____

In the book of Lamentations, the prophet Jeremiah makes it clear that God's compassions are as dependable as His faithfulness. Every new day brings new compassions from the Lord.

Anguish and Hope (Lamentations 3:19–27)

¹⁹ Remember my affliction and roaming,
The wormwood and the gall.
²⁰ My soul still remembers
And sinks within me.
²¹ This I recall to my mind,
Therefore I have hope.

²² Through the LORD's mercies we are not consumed,
Because His compassions fail not.
²³ They are new every morning;
Great is Your faithfulness.

125

24 "The LORD is my portion," says my soul,
"Therefore I hope in Him!"

25 The LORD is good to those who wait for Him,
To the soul who seeks Him.
26 It is good that one should hope and wait quietly
For the salvation of the LORD.
27 It is good for a man to bear
The yoke in his youth.

---

7. Jeremiah began this chapter in Lamentations by voicing his hopelessness because of the affliction God allowed him to suffer (see verses 1–18). In this passage, his perspective shifts. What happens when he recalls the Lord's faithful mercies (see verses 21–24)?

_____

_____

_____

_____

_____

_____

_____

_____

_____

_____

_____

_____

_____

8. Jeremiah responds to the suffering he is enduring by affirming the Lord's goodness. He then provides reasons for why suffering ("the yoke") is "good for a man to bear." How can suffering in the life of a believer be viewed as something good (see verses 25–27)?

_____

_____

_____

_____

_____

_____

REVIEWING THE STORY

The Lord's faithfulness had powered the apostle Paul's ministry. In this closing section of his letter, he boldly asks the Thessalonian believers to pray for him, knowing that God would hear and answer their requests. Paul then shares his confidence with the Thessalonians, giving them the courage to embark on their own ministries without worrying about attacks from the enemy of God's work. Paul encourages them to stay active in their faith and instructs them to avoid those who have decided to drop out of active service and idly wait for the Lord to return.

9. What does Paul ask the Thessalonian believers to pray that the Lord would do for him in his ministry (see 2 Thessalonians 3:1–2)?

_____

_____

_____

_____

_____

_____

10. Because of God's faithfulness, how does Paul feel about the prospects for spiritual growth among the Thessalonians (see 2 Thessalonians 3:4)?

_____

_____

_____

_____

11. What does Paul encourage the Thessalonians to do, in terms of their work ethic (see 2 Thessalonians 3:7–8)?

_____

_____

_____

_____

12. Why did Paul toil day and night when he could have used his apostolic authority to get support from the Thessalonians (see 2 Thessalonians 3:8–9)?

_____

_____

_____

_____

APPLYING THE MESSAGE

13. What are some ways that God has proven His faithfulness to you?

_____

_____

_____

_____

14. How can you remind yourself of God's faithfulness the next time you are tempted to doubt Him or to turn elsewhere for guidance?

_____

_____

_____

_____

_____

REFLECTING ON THE MEANING

In this section of Paul's second letter to the Thessalonians, he prays that God will *direct* the believers' hearts into the love of God and the patience of Christ (see 2 Thessalonians 3:5). The Greek word translated *direct* in this verse actually means "to make straight." Paul is thus asking God to remove any barriers in the believers' lives that would cause their way to become crooked. His prayer is for God to remove any obstacles that threaten to block their progress.

God wants to do the same in the lives of people today. He wants to remove any barriers that may be blocking them from experiencing His love. Just imagine what would happen if you were to pray, "Lord, I have a friend who is struggling in the faith. Today, I ask that You would remove any barriers that are keeping my friend from growing closer to You. Please make the way straight so my friend can experience Your presence in a new and fresh way." If you prayed this prayer, you would see the hand of God move in that person's life.

Likewise, if a friend were to pray that prayer for *you*, you would see any obstacles to your spiritual growth begin to melt away. Perhaps this is a relationship that has kept you from growing. Or a commitment that has monopolized your schedule. Or a problem that has been so overwhelming that you haven't been able to focus on anything else. God can remove all these obstacles to growth—and can also create new avenues for you to discover His will.

JOURNALING YOUR RESPONSE

What are some barriers in your life that might be keeping you from growing in your faith and seeking after God? How can you remove these barriers?

THE IMPORTANCE OF WORK

2 Thessalonians 3:10–18

GETTING STARTED

What are some of the types of work that you like to do—whether for a career or a hobby?

_____

_____

_____

_____

_____

_____

_____

_____

_____

_____

_____

_____

_____

_____

_____

_____

_____

_____

SETTING THE STAGE

It is interesting that in Scripture, the people God called to serve Him were often busy with their own work when that call came. Moses was caring for sheep. Joshua was Moses' servant before he became Moses' successor. Gideon was threshing wheat. David was caring for his father's sheep when he was anointed for kingship by the prophet Samuel. Jesus called four fishermen, who were tending their nets, to serve as disciples. He Himself worked as a carpenter.

Work has an important role in God's plan and purpose for our lives. Work is divinely intended to give us a sense of self-worth. Even as far back as the Garden of Eden, the Lord was providing gainful employment for His creation: "Out of the ground the Lord God formed every beast of the field and every bird of the air, and brought them to Adam to see what he would call them. And whatever Adam called each living creature, that was its name" (Genesis 2:19).

Work is valuable because it gives a sense of meaning to life. When we are working, we feel a sense of accomplishment. When we are unable to work, we feel out of sorts. It can be disturbing, and psychologically upsetting, to be without work. For this reason, we should thank God every day that He has given us something productive to do—something that makes a difference in the lives of others and gives us a sense of fulfillment.

Paul, for his part, worked as a tentmaker even after receiving his call from God to be an apostle of the gospel. He worked on the side, wherever he went, to support his ministry. So, he was uniquely qualified to instruct the Thessalonians on the subject of work when he discovered that many of the believers in the church were neglecting their duties. They were using the imminence of the Lord's return as an excuse to be lazy.

Paul addressed this issue in his first letter to the church when he wrote, "Aspire to lead a quiet life, to mind your own business, and to work with your own hands, as we commanded you, that you may walk properly toward those who are outside, and that you may lack nothing" (1 Thessalonians 4:11–12). However, as is often the case, the lesson didn't quite take root. So, in this final chapter of his second letter, he tackles the subject once again.

EXPLORING THE TEXT

Warning Against Idleness (2 Thessalonians 3:10–13)

¹⁰ For even when we were with you, we commanded you this: If anyone will not work, neither shall he eat. ¹¹ For we hear that there are some who walk among you in a disorderly manner, not working at all, but are busybodies. ¹² Now those who are such we command and exhort through our Lord Jesus Christ that they work in quietness and eat their own bread.

¹³ But as for you, brethren, do not grow weary in doing good.

1. Paul had evidently received visitors from Thessalonica who reported that some of the believers in the city were spending their time not working but rather meddling in other people's lives. How had Paul previously addressed the issue with the church (see verses 10–11)?

2. Paul reminds the believers of their shared faith in Jesus Christ and gently appeals to them to avoid living idly and as busybodies. How does Paul encourage the believers to live in light of the problem of idleness in the church (verses 12–13)?

_____

_____

_____

_____

_____

Salutation and Benediction (2 Thessalonians 3:14–18)

14 And if anyone does not obey our word in this epistle, note that person and do not keep company with him, that he may be ashamed. 15 Yet do not count him as an enemy, but admonish him as a brother.

16 Now may the Lord of peace Himself give you peace always in every way. The Lord be with you all.

17 The salutation of Paul with my own hand, which is a sign in every epistle; so I write.

18 The grace of our Lord Jesus Christ be with you all. Amen.

3. Paul tells the Thessalonian believers to deal firmly with those in their midst who are lazy. Yet he models compassion in his teaching regarding how to treat lazy people. How should believers deal with other believers who choose idleness over work (see verses 14–15)?

_____

_____

_____

_____

_____

4. Paul moves from commanding the believers to praying for them. For what does Paul pray as it relates to the church? What role does prayer play in reconciling hard workers and idlers in the body of Christ (see verse 16)?

_____

_____

_____

_____

_____

_____

GOING DEEPER

King Solomon, and others who contributed to the writing of the book of Proverbs, understood the importance of work—in our relationship with the Lord, in society, and in our self-image. He offers a particularly stark warning against laziness in the following passage.

Warnings Against Idleness (Proverbs 24:30–34)

30 I went by the field of the lazy man,

And by the vineyard of the man devoid of understanding;

31 And there it was, all overgrown with thorns;

Its surface was covered with nettles;

Its stone wall was broken down.

32 When I saw it, I considered it well;

I looked on it and received instruction:

33 A little sleep, a little slumber,

A little folding of the hands to rest;

34 So shall your poverty come like a prowler,

And your need like an armed man.

5. The writers of the book of Proverbs frequently commented on the consequences of neglecting to work diligently. What images does the writer use in this passage to portray the negative effects of laziness (see verses 30–31)?

_____

_____

_____

_____

_____

_____

_____

6. The writer of Proverbs calls his readers to carefully weigh the consequences of living idly. Why is it risky to underestimate the importance of work (see verses 32–34)?

_____

_____

_____

_____

_____

_____

_____

The apostle Paul recognized that believers in the church needed to hold one another accountable in the faith. This included dealing with problem issues—such as idleness—when they arose. In Paul's letter to the Galatians, he reminds the believers to lovingly confront brothers and sisters when they sin, but to be careful to set a good example in the faith in their own lives.

Reaping What You Sow (Galatians 6:1–10)

[1] Brethren, if a man is overtaken in any trespass, you who are spiritual restore such a one in a spirit of gentleness, considering yourself lest you also be tempted. [2] Bear one another's burdens, and so fulfill the law of Christ. [3] For if anyone thinks himself to be something, when he is nothing, he deceives himself. [4] But let each one examine his own work, and then he will have rejoicing in himself alone, and not in another. [5] For each one shall bear his own load.

[6] Let him who is taught the word share in all good things with him who teaches.

[7] Do not be deceived, God is not mocked; for whatever a man sows, that he will also reap. [8] For he who sows to his flesh will of the flesh reap corruption, but he who sows to the Spirit will of the Spirit reap everlasting life. [9] And let us not grow weary while doing good, for in due season we shall reap if we do not lose heart. [10] Therefore, as we have opportunity, let us do good to all, especially to those who are of the household of faith.

7. Paul warns the Galatians of the temptation for believers to act superior to others believers. How does he want them to confront their brothers and sisters who have fallen into temptation? How could they keep from falling into the same traps (see verses 1–5)?

8. Paul writes, "Whatever a man sows, that he will also reap" (verse 7). Those who are idle and refuse to work will reap nothing, while those who work diligently will reap the benefits of their work. How does Paul call the believers to work (or to "sow")? What are the benefits of work that pleases God (see verses 7–10)?

_____

_____

_____

_____

_____

_____

REVIEWING THE STORY

Paul closes his second letter to the Thessalonians by emphasizing the importance of work. In doing so, he is responding to those in the congregation who have given up working for a life of idleness. They had reasoned that if Jesus were returning soon, there was no reason for them to work. Paul urges the other Thessalonian believers to separate themselves from such idle brothers and sisters. He ends the letter with his traditional benediction and salutations.

9. What disappointing news had Paul received about some of the people in the Thessalonian church (see 2 Thessalonians 3:11)?

_____

_____

_____

_____

_____

10. How did idleness lead to other problems in the church
(see 2 Thessalonians 3:11)?

_____

_____

_____

_____

_____

11. What is Paul's intended result in advising the Thessalonian
believers to refuse to keep company with those who are disobedient to
God's Word (see 2 Thessalonians 3:14)?

_____

_____

_____

_____

_____

_____

12. What does Paul do to make sure that the Thessalonian
believers will not be deceived again by someone posing as him
(see 2 Thessalonians 3:17)?

_____

_____

_____

_____

_____

_____

APPLYING THE MESSAGE

13. How does Paul's teaching influence your work ethic and your attitude toward work?

_____

_____

_____

_____

_____

_____

_____

_____

_____

14. How can you use your work ethic—and your work—as part of your witness for Christ?

_____

_____

_____

_____

_____

_____

_____

_____

_____

REFLECTING ON THE MEANING

Paul's final command to the Thessalonians is to withdraw from any believer who is leading a disorderly life. "But we command you, brethren, in the name of our Lord Jesus Christ, that you withdraw from every borother who walks disorderly and not according to the tradition which you received from us" (2 Thessalonians 3:6). Disorderly people, if not dealt with appropriately, can cause conflicts and divisions within a church. Paul desires unity among the body of Christ. So, his words to the Thessalonians provide valuable insights on how to deal with such individuals.

First, we are to acknowledge their conduct. Paul says we are to "note that person" (2 Thessalonians 3:14). Those in the church are not to ignore the disorderly person but to take steps to deal with the issue. This typically begins with a conversation with a leader or pastor, which serves as warning to the person that he or she is causing disunity in the body of Christ and should immediately cease the disorderly conduct.

Second, we are to avoid their company (see verse 14). We are to refrain from associating with the person in a manner that would allow him or her to poison our own spirit. This may mean not going to some meetings the person attends or not being a "friend" with that person on social media. As Paul wrote in another letter, "Evil company corrupts good habits" (1 Corinthians 15:33). We can't allow anyone to influence and corrupt our own behavior.

Third, we are to admonish them as Christians. Paul says we "do not count him as an enemy, but admonish him as a brother" (verse 15). We are to confront the person as a Christian, treating him or her in a manner that leads to repentance and restoration. As we do this, we guard our spirits so we do not become sinful in the process of confronting the person. We go to the person out of love and because we know that if he or she continues moving in this direction, there will ultimately be negative consequences for the conduct.

This is a draining passage of Scripture, because it deals with an unpleasant topic. But Paul's final benediction brings some needed relief. In the final verses, we find God's prescription for living in the days prior to Christ's return: the peace of God, and the grace of God, mediated through the representative of God (see 2 Thessalonians 3:16–18). May that be your experience in the church where you serve the Lord as you wait for His glorious appearing!

JOURNALING YOUR RESPONSE

How would you want someone to confront you if you were "disorderly"?

LEADER'S GUIDE

Thank you for choosing to lead your group through this study from Dr. David Jeremiah on *The Letters of 1 & 2 Thessalonians*. Being a group leader has its own rewards, and it is our prayer that your walk with the Lord will deepen through this experience. During the twelve lessons in this study, you and your group will read selected passages from these letters, explore key themes in them based on teachings from Dr. Jeremiah, and review questions that will encourage group discussion. There are multiple components in this section that can help you structure your lessons and discussion time, so please be sure to read and consider each one.

Before You Begin

Before your first meeting, make sure you and your group are well-versed with the content of the lesson. Group members should have their own copy of *The Letters of 1 & 2 Thessalonians* study guide prior to the first meeting so they can follow along and record their answers, thoughts, and insights. After the first week, you may wish to assign the study guide lesson as homework prior to the group meeting and then use the meeting time to discuss the content in the lesson.

To ensure everyone has a chance to participate in the discussion, the ideal size for a group is around eight to ten people. If there are more than ten people, break up the bigger group into smaller subgroups. Make sure the members are committed to participating each week, as this will help create stability and help you better prepare the structure of the meeting.

At the beginning of each week's study, start with the opening Getting Started question to introduce the topic you will be discussing. The members should answer briefly, as the goal is just for them to have an idea of the subject in their minds as you go over the lesson. This will allow the members to become engaged and ready to interact with the rest of the group.

After reviewing the lesson, try to initiate a free-flowing discussion. Invite group members to bring questions and insights they may have discovered to the next meeting, especially if they were unsure of the meaning of some parts of the lesson. Be prepared to discuss how biblical truth applies to the world we live in today.

Weekly Preparation

As the group leader, here are a few things that you can do to prepare for each meeting:

- *Be thoroughly familiar with the material in the lesson.* Make sure that you understand the content of each lesson so you know how to structure the group time and are prepared to lead the group discussion.

- *Decide, ahead of time, which questions you want to discuss.* Depending on how much time you have each week, you may not be able to reflect on every question. Select specific questions that you feel will evoke the best discussion.

- *Take prayer requests.* At the end of your discussion, take prayer requests from your group members and then pray for one another.

Structuring the Discussion Time

There are several ways to structure the duration of the study. You can choose to cover each lesson individually, for a total of twelve weeks of group meetings, or you can combine two lessons together per week, for a total of six weeks of group meetings. The following charts illustrate these options:

TWELVE-WEEK FORMAT

Week	Lessons Covered	Reading
1	A Dynamic Church	*1 Thessalonians 1:1–10*
2	Hallmarks of Authentic Ministry	*1 Thessalonians 2:1–12*
3	A Shared Experience of Suffering	*1 Thessalonians 2:13–20*
4	Growing Up in the Faith	*1 Thessalonians 3:1–13*
5	The Call to a Holy Life	*1 Thessalonians 4:1–18*
6	The Believer and the Tribulation	*1 Thessalonians 5:1–11*
7	Anticipating Jesus' Return	*1 Thessalonians 5:12–28*
8	Standing Strong in Tribulation	*2 Thessalonians 1:1–12*
9	The Antichrist Is Coming	*2 Thessalonians 2:1–8*
10	Truth for Troubled Times	*2 Thessalonians 2:9–17*
11	God Is Always Faithful	*2 Thessalonians 3:1–9*
12	The Importance of Work	*2 Thessalonians 3:10–18*

SIX-WEEK FORMAT

Week	Lessons Covered	Reading
1	A Dynamic Church / Hallmarks of Authentic Ministry	*1 Thessalonians 1:1–2:12*
2	A Shared Experience of Suffering / Growing Up in the Faith	*1 Thessalonians 2:13–3:13*
3	The Call to a Holy Life / The Believer and the Tribulation	*1 Thessalonians 4:1–5:11*
4	Anticipating Jesus' Return / Standing Strong in Tribulation	*1 Thessalonians 5:12– 2 Thessalonians 1:12*
5	The Antichrist Is Coming / Truth for Troubled Times	*2 Thessalonians 2:1–17*
6	God Is Always Faithful / The Importance of Work	*2 Thessalonians 3:1–18*

In regard to organizing your time when planning your group Bible study, the following two schedules, for sixty minutes and ninety minutes, can give you a structure for the lesson:

Section	60 Minutes	90 Minutes
Welcome: Members arrive and get settled	5 minutes	10 minutes
Getting Started Question: Prepares the group for interacting with one another	10 minutes	10 minutes
Message: Review the lesson	15 minutes	25 minutes
Discussion: Discuss questions in the lesson	25 minutes	35 minutes
Review and Prayer: Review the key points of the lesson and have a closing time of prayer	5 minutes	10 minutes

As the group leader, it is up to you to keep track of the time and keep things moving according to your schedule. If your group is having a good discussion, don't feel the need to stop and move on to the next question. Remember, the purpose is to pull together ideas and share unique insights on the lesson. Encourage everyone to participate, but don't be concerned if certain group members are more quiet. They may just be internally reflecting on the questions and need time to process their ideas before they can share them.

GROUP DYNAMICS

Leading a group study can be a rewarding experience for you and your group members—but that doesn't mean there won't be challenges. Certain members may feel uncomfortable discussing topics that they consider very personal and might be afraid of being called on. Some members might have disagreements on specific issues. To help prevent these scenarios, consider the following ground rules:

- If someone has a question that may seem off topic, suggest that it be discussed at another time, or ask the group if they are okay with addressing that topic.

- If someone asks a question you don't know the answer to, confess that you don't know and move on. If you feel comfortable, invite other group members to give their opinions or share their comments based on personal experience.
- If you feel like a couple of people are talking much more than others, direct questions to people who may not have shared yet. You could even ask the more dominating members to help draw out the quiet ones.
- When there is a disagreement, encourage the group members to process the matter in love. Invite members from opposing sides to evaluate their opinions and consider the ideas of the other members. Lead the group through Scripture that addresses the topic, and look for common ground.

When issues arise, encourage your group to think of Scripture: "Love one another" (John 13:34), "If it is possible, as much as it depends on you, live peaceably with all men" (Romans 12:18), and, "Be swift to hear, slow to speak, slow to wrath" (James 1:19).

ABOUT

Dr. David Jeremiah and Turning Point

Dr. David Jeremiah is the founder of Turning Point, a ministry committed to providing Christians with sound Bible teaching relevant to today's changing times through radio and television broadcasts, audio series, books, and live events. Dr. Jeremiah's teaching on topics such as family, prayer, worship, angels, and biblical prophecy forms the foundation of Turning Point.

David and his wife, Donna, reside in El Cajon, California, where he serves as the senior pastor of Shadow Mountain Community Church. David and Donna have four children and twelve grandchildren.

In 1982, Dr. Jeremiah brought the same solid teaching to San Diego television that he shares weekly with his congregation. Shortly thereafter, Turning Point expanded its ministry to radio. Dr. Jeremiah's inspiring messages can now be heard worldwide on radio, television, and the internet. Because Dr. Jeremiah desires to know his listening audience, he travels nationwide, holding ministry rallies and spiritual enrichment conferences that touch the hearts and lives of many people.

Dr. Jeremiah has authored numerous books, including *Escape the Coming Night* (Revelation), *The Handwriting on the Wall* (Daniel), *God in You* (Holy Spirit), *When Your World Falls Apart*, *Slaying the Giants in Your Life*, *My Heart's Desire*, *Hope for Today*, *Captured by Grace*, *Signs of Life*, *What in the World Is Going On?*, *The Coming Economic Armageddon*, *I Never Thought I'd See the Day!*, *God Loves You: He Always Has—He Always Will*, *Agents of the Apocalypse*, *Agents of Babylon*, *Revealing the Mysteries of Heaven*, *People Are Asking . . . Is This the End?*, *A Life Beyond Amazing*, *Overcomer*, *The Book of Signs*, and *Everything You Need*.